Guide!
No Perfectin

change your life
DAILY JOURNAL

a daily journal experience to balance your life
physically, emotionally, spiritually & mentally

BECKY
Becky
TIRABASSI
change your life®

B E C K Y
T I R A B A S S I
change your life ®

change your life
DAILY JOURNAL

Most of us gravitate to...

> ### *gimmicks,*
> ### *concepts,*
> ### *plans, or*
> ### *institutions*

that promise change, because we are looking for the quickest and easiest way to...

- improve our relationships,
- advance in business,
- increase our income,
- achieve emotional happiness and/or,
- receive spiritual wholeness and healing!

But unfortunately, whether we are searching for physical, emotional, financial, relational or spiritual change, our search often ends in defeat.

Unless we possess effective time management skills, or have been mentored by strong, disciplined people, we are more prone to give up or cave in to negative thoughts and criticism, than to actually achieve our goals.

If up until now you have only hoped to master concepts such as,

"fulfilling your dreams,"

"becoming successful,"

"being consistent,"

"reaching your goals," or

"effectively managing your time,"

then the **Becky Tirabassi change your life, Inc®
Balanced Life Philosophy** is for you!

change your life is not simply a promise-in-theory,
but a proven, practical, balanced life philosophy for daily living,
which provides on-going motivation through the internet,
television, seminars, videos, audio tapes, and books. The
change your life Daily Journal is the place to work
through and record your changes. In fact, I predict -- if daily
used -- this journal will effectively and powerfully bring balance,
hope, healing, success -- and change -- into your life.

change
your
life
daily

the premise

From 1971 until 1976, I was an alcoholic. In a dramatic turn of events, I had a life-changing encounter with God that re-routed my life from a path of self-destruction to a path of fulfillment, self-respect, and personal achievement!

Within days of that encounter, almost every physical and spiritual aspect of my life began to change. My obvious and destructive habits were replaced with powerful, ethical disciplines and new, moral patterns and desires. After a year of sobriety and recovery, I married a wonderful man and a year later had a child. Immediately, I began giving back to the community by mentoring and coaching high school students, encouraging them to balance their lives physically, emotionally, spiritually, and mentally.

But even though many physical and spiritual characteristics of mine had changed, the previous patterns that had always plagued my personality, such as competitiveness, manipulation, tardiness, procrastination, and lack of organization, continued to undermine my personal success, as well as hinder my emotional health and growth.

In February of 1984, I attended a professional youth worker's conference. It was during the powerful messages that I realized I was burned out in my job, having difficulties in my personal and professional relationships, and jealous of others' successes. At that conference, I became...

> aware of,
>
> honest about, and
>
> disgusted with

my lack of fulfillment and unhappiness. I acknowledged that my repeated excuses and undisciplined efforts had caused me to waste my inherent God-given talents and squander my potential for success.

I was desperate for change, but because so many aspects of my life needed revision, I had no idea where to begin! One thing was certain: I was ready and willing to take *any* step and make any change that would bring relief to my discouragement, and significant, speedy improvements to my life.

After a Saturday workshop, in the presence of another person, I admitted I needed to change, asked God to help me, and made a decision to journal for one hour every day for the rest of my life.

Journaling became the practical skill that was necessary to turn my undisciplined life into a balanced life -- physically, emotionally, spiritually, and mentally!

At that convention in February of 1984, I made a decision to journal for one hour every day for the rest of my life. An organized notebook became the place where I wrote and recorded my prayers, dreams, hopes, struggles, anxieties, accomplishments and thoughts -- on a daily basis. This tool allowed me to...

> see,
>
> experience,
>
> expect,
>
> and record changes in
>
> my personality,
>
> financial status,
>
> relationships,
>
> spiritual growth,
>
> emotional health,
>
> physical fitness, and
>
> use of time.

Through journaling, I have been successfully and methodically fulfilling my dreams and reaching my goals.

Journaling has given me:

- a *place* to set and achieve realistic goals,
- the *courage* to face up to the truth about my past and make amends in my relationships,
- *accountability* in my finances (to give, save and spend); and
- *organization* in my daily life, so that I plan for my future in increments of today, 1 week, 1 month, 90 days, 1 year and beyond.

Since I have been recording, writing, praying, meditating, and goal setting for over 16 years, I have been able to track and validate how my struggles have eventually turned into successes.

By encouraging you to use the **change your life Daily Journal** and to follow the **Becky Tirabassi change your life, Inc® Balanced Life Philosophy** , I am confident that you will receive the incentive, courage, resources and skills that you need to change your life!

the process

In my search for healing, health, and fulfillment, I have found that change cannot be achieved by focusing solely on one area, but by balancing the physical, emotional, spiritual and mental areas of one's life.

By making daily journal entries on each of the four "balanced life" pages:

Physical,

Emotional,

Spiritual and

Mental,

as well as using the organizational section of this journal,

Calendar,

I believe that you will be encouraged, motivated and inspired to develop, pursue, plan, work through, improve -- and ultimately, change -- every area of your life! In fact, I am confident that you will look back in one year -- or even in one month -- and find that many aspects of your life have changed!

I predict that your eating habits and exercise patterns will become more healthy and consistent! In addition, I have no doubt that you will experience improved emotional health. I also believe that your relationships with others and with God will have changed and improved. And in a short time, I contend that you will slowly, but surely and successfully achieve the personal, financial, and business goals that you set.

Have you been looking for these kinds of changes in your life?

If it is your desire to change the areas of your life that resemble chaos, insecurity, anxiety, workaholism (or any "ism" for that matter) and to turn an unbalanced life into a balanced life, then join me! Take the next few months of your life and *begin* the process of developing positive patterns toward a balanced life through the **change your life Daily Journal** and other **Becky Tirabassi change your life, Inc**® resources.

your part

Let's assume that you make -- and keep -- appointments with other people. In order to change your life, I am asking you to make a daily appointment with yourself in the **c h a n g e y o u r l i f e Daily Journal**.

On each journal page, you have the opportunity to change your life -- one day at a time -- by recording your plans, intentions, hopes, deepest desires, thoughts and dreams! My only request is that you make at least one entry on each of the four balanced life pages every day, and transfer any "to do's" to the **Mental** and **Calendar** page of your journal.

I have placed the journal pages in a particular order, but if you prefer to start your day in the spiritual or emotional or mental pages, I encourage you to do so!

I believe that your ability to see your life change by using the **c h a n g e y o u r l i f e Daily Journal** is dependent upon your daily commitment to journal in each of the balanced life pages -- no matter how comfortable or convenient this may be to you.

the plan

Each balanced life page is divided into two sections that will give you eight practical ways to change your life. **I call these the 8 Daily To Do's.**

On the **Physical** journal page, record daily how you intend to *Eat Right* and *Exercise Regularly*.

On the **Emotional** journal page, you have an opportunity to daily *Forgive* and *Give*.

On the **Spiritual** journal page, you can record two-way conversations where you *Talk to God* and *Listen to God.*

And on the **Mental** journal page, you are encouraged to *Detail Your Day* and *Define Your Dream*.

Ideally, these journal pages will cause you to think and plan, dream and design, then later turn these ideas into "to do's." You will begin to see your life change when you transfer the ideas and thoughts from your journal pages to the **Mental** and **Calendar** pages of the **c h a n g e   y o u r   l i f e Daily Journal**. Note: Your total time commitment in the journal is only between 15 and 20 minutes!

For insured success, I suggest that you make yourself accountable to at least one other person. I asked a small group of friends if they would come to my house for a **c h a n g e y o u r   l i f e Group**, held once a week for one hour. Though we were all at different ages and stages of our lives, we shared our goals, progress and struggles in each of the four balanced life areas. We laughed and cried, grew close, were encouraged, and truly watched our lives change for the better!

Eat Right

As recommended by most effective eating programs, keeping a written record of what you eat will lead to success, if you are consistent and honest in your record keeping.

The **c h a n g e   y o u r   l i f e Daily Journal** makes this discipline simple to follow and easy to live with. Recording what you plan to eat on a given day is the first step to success. Thinking about what possible pitfalls might occur in your day can give you the insight and courage to recognize and avoid temptation.

Following a healthy eating plan that suits your lifestyle and is recommended by your doctor is the best way to feel great and see results.

Doing your own research, or subscribing to a fitness or health magazine is an additional way to make informed and educated eating choices, and will give you an even greater opportunity for success. By integrating healthy foods and good eating habits into your lifestyle, your family will be positively effected, as well!

Exercise Regularly

You don't need to be an expert in anatomy or physiology to see that regular exercise makes a difference in one's body weight and shape, as well as in one's stress level and cardiovascular fitness.

The question has never been, "DOES exercise work," but "HOW can I get myself to exercise?"

For me, a fitness program has to be fun, and include either companions or music. Whether I ride a mountain bike outdoors with a friend, or go to the gym for a Step class, I have discovered which workouts keep me returning for more. But for one of my friends, exercise has to be challenging. We are all different. The key to your individual success will be to design and follow a fitness program that fits your personality, lifestyle, and priorities.

In order to see changes in your body, or just to maintain your weight, you should plan to workout 3 or 4 times each week. Planning your workouts one week in advance is the best way to achieve that goal. In the planning stage, it is important to be realistic about your family priorities and work commitments. Being flexible and having an alternate set of plans for those unexpected, but inevitable interruptions is essential for long-term success!

Forgive

Having experienced alcoholism first hand, I know that recovery from addiction is a life long, on-going process. But, I have also lived long enough to realize that the entire human race is made up of imperfect people with their own flaws and shortcomings. I haven't met a person yet who is faultless! And I haven't been involved in one relationship that was perfect! At varying times and in a variety of ways, we hurt, offend, injure, or misuse people whom we love and those we don't even know.

I believe, in order to bring the emotional area of your life into balance, you must forgive others and yourself on a daily basis. If you are honest about your own imperfections, you will become less judgmental and critical of others. As you extend forgiveness, you will react and respond to others with humility and kindness, rather than with selfishness or anger.

In all honesty, the emotional area of my life has been my greatest challenge! The most practical way I have found to bring healing and growth to this area has been through journaling. Within the safe confines of my journal, I have been able to confront my personality flaws, admit my anger and resentments, and forgive others.

I would encourage you to do the same!

change
your
life
daily

Give

Perhaps this section of the **c h a n g e   y o u r   l i f e Daily Journal** is the most enjoyable section for me. We all agree that giving out of habit or expectation is admirable. But, giving to fill a need, make amends, or cause someone to be better off than they were before is life changing for both the recipient and the giver!

The practice of daily looking for and thinking of ways to give to someone who has less than you do, or needs something that you have, or can't make ends meet without your help is revolutionary.

Since beginning the **c h a n g e   y o u r   l i f e Daily Journal,** I have been amazed at how many unique ways I have thought of to help another, go beyond what was expected, or really make a difference in someone's life or situation. Perhaps this section has changed me the most because I tend to be more selfish than selfless. But, when given the opportunity, I've been jumping at the chance to give!

This section encourages you to daily consider how you can give of your time or talents. You will be stretched and you will be surprised at how good it feels to give!

Talk to God

You are not alone if you struggle with believing that God exists, or that you can have a conversation with Him! But I have found that talking to God, whom you can't see, is similar to communicating with an unseen friend on the phone, or through the mail, or over the internet. Though you can't see them, you believe that they are somewhere out there, will hear you, and will respond to you.

I believe that when you talk to God, you are talking to Someone who not only exists, but who loves you, knows you, and has the ability and power to help you. The goal of the **Spiritual** journal page is to encourage you to have a daily, casual, two-way conversation with the person of God.

In the journal space provided, write a letter to God, expressing your thoughts and concerns. Be honest with Him. Share your feelings and your fears. Admit your struggles and ask for His help. Talk to Him about others who need His help, as well. Thank Him for something or someone positive in your day.

Keeping a record of your conversations with God is a wonderful way to chart your spiritual journey!

s
p
i
r
i
t
u
a
l

Listen to God

Listening to God is not meant to be magical or mystical. God has made it attainable for you to hear His voice by giving you His word, the Bible. Anyone, of any race, can know of God's unchanging love, power, and plan, simply by reading the Bible.

The Bible includes history, poetry and parables that detail how God loves all people, interacts with them, speaks to them and has a plan for eternal life. Without reading the Bible, you limit your knowledge of God and your ability to hear His voice. By reading the Bible daily, you increase your ability to know and understand Him.

In order for me to hear God's voice on a daily basis, I have made it a practice to read a Bible that is divided into 365 days! For over 10 years, this has made reading the entire Bible in one year a manageable and easy task. The **c h a n g e y o u r l i f e Daily Bible** is the entire Bible divided into 365 days and is designed to be used with the **c h a n g e y o u r l i f e Daily Journal.**

If you are just beginning to listen to God or to read the Bible, simply locate today's date in the **c h a n g e y o u r l i f e Daily Bible** and read! To connect with God, I suggest that you underline any verse or verses that stand out, touch your heart, or give you direction, correction, and encouragement! Then, in the **Listen to God** space of the **Spiritual** journal page, record those verses, using your own words and thoughts!

change
your
life
daily

Detail Your Day

Taking the time to transfer your journal entries from the **Physical, Emotional, and Spiritual** balanced life pages to this page will insure that each day is manageable and productive! You can think of this page as a worksheet or an official To-do list. You can carry it with you to guide your day, or you can transfer this list into your already existing daily planner.

This page has a purpose: to help you successfully lead an effective, balanced life. As you set and keep your appointments, make your phone calls, write your letters, and meet your deadlines, you will begin to feel balance in your life. You will notice that your relationships become more healthy, your physical fitness will improve, and you might even find that your income increases and your debt reduces as a result of using the **c h a n g e   y o u r   l i f e Daily Journal**!

Soon this page will be proof that balance comes to those who take the time to plan and have the tenacity to persevere.

Define Your Dream

Dreams can, and do become a reality for those who persevere. It may not happen in the time frame you prefer, or in the way that you imagined, but your dream is more likely to become a reality, if you don't give up!

A dream might begin with an idea or a desire to fill a need. If you keep searching, trying, knocking on doors, believing in and revising your dream, you will find a way to be successful.

In this area, your only task is to dream and brainstorm. This space never has to be seen by anyone. Lack of money or negative criticism can't touch your dream. Therefore, don't discount any ideas! No one can reject you.

Observe, as the days go by, if your dream or idea grows stronger or weaker. I once heard a speaker say, "A dream that won't go away is from God!" So, don't try to talk yourself into or out of an idea. Hold on to your dream. And don't be afraid to dream big.

Use this space to take one more step toward a dream that is in your heart that won't go away.

calendar

The **c h a n g e   y o u r   l i f e Daily Journal** includes two month-at-a-glance **Calendars**. It is important, as you begin to plan your day, to look at your whole week, as well as the entire month. The monthly **Calendar** allows you to see the complete picture, so that you better manage and prioritize each day, week, and month. In addition, this overview allows you to quickly notice when your planning is not realistic or when your life is in danger of being out of balance.

On a daily basis, each journal page might include one or more items that should be transferred to the **Mental** page or **Calendar**. Your life will become more balanced as you learn to adjust your schedule to reflect your priorities. By placing reminders on your **Calendar**, in advance of a deadline, you will not forget important dates, run out of time, or be tempted to procrastinate. If you diligently use this method or incorporate it into an already existing system, I am confident that you will accomplish more each month than ever before!

Using a calendar takes practice. Becoming an effective time-manager takes time. Because time is so valuable, how and with whom you spend it should be a reflection of your priorities.

If you need extra space to record ongoing dreams, thoughts, goals, ideas prayer requests or lists, there is one page at the end of this **c h a n g e   y o u r   l i f e Daily Journal** is just for you!

prepare to begin

Here are a few final tips to help you have a successful start as you begin the **change your life Daily Journal.**

1   Each day consists of four balanced life pages -- **Physical, Emotional, Spiritual, and Mental**. There is a blank line next to the word **date** at the top of each page. On the day in which you begin the Journal, place the number 1 or today's date in the **date** space of all four of the balanced life pages -- then fill in your journal entries.

2   Next, fill in the month-at-a-glance **Calendar** to make it current.

3   After making your first journal entries on each of the four balanced life pages, transfer any "to-do's" to the **Calendar**.

4   Repeat this process every day! **You have 60 days of journal pages!**

5   If you miss a day, or even a few days, don't try to catch up, just begin where you left off.

6   To help you to quickly locate where you left off in the Journal each day, use a favorite bookmark to mark your place. Even a paper clip, or a fold on the **date** corners will give you a beginning and ending point.

your promise

To make a written commitment to use the
c h a n g e   y o u r   l i f e Daily Journal,
please mail, fax, or email this (or a similar) sheet to:

> **Becky Tirabassi c h a n g e   y o u r   l i f e ,Inc.**®
> Box 9672, Newport Beach, Ca. 92660
>
> Phone: 1-800-444-6189
> Fax: 1-949-644-8044
> email: cyl@changeyourlifedaily.com
> www.changeyourlifedaily.com

Date: _____

Name: _____

Address:_____

_____

Email: _____

Promise: _____

_____

_____

My Accountability Partner: _____

In 60 days, an exciting letter of encouragement
will be sent to you!

product order form

Title	Qty	Price
Change Your Life Book	_____	$13.00
change your life Daily Journal	_____	$17.00
change your life Daily Bible	_____	$18.00
change your life Audio Tape	_____	$15.00
change your life Walking Audio Series	_____	$25.00
Making Fitness Fun Fitness Video	_____	$20.00

Subtotal:

Sales Tax (*in CA only*)   subtotal x 7.5%   _____

Shipping: $2.50 *per item* $2.50 x _____   _____

Handling Charge $2.00

Grand Total:

Name _____

Address _____

City _____ State ____ Zip _____

Phone _____

Email _____

Visa, MC, AMEX or Discover # _____

Exp. _____

Becky Tirabassi change your life, Inc.®
To order by mail:
Send check, money order, VISA, M/C, AMEX or Discover # and Exp. date to:

Becky Tirabassi change your life, Inc.®
Box 9672, Newport Beach, CA 92660

To order by fax: **1-949-644-8044**
To order by phone: **1-800-444-6189**
To order by internet: **www.changeyourlifedaily.com**

change
your
life
daily

date _____

eat right

- understand your own body type, genetics, metabolism, etc.
- design a healthy, "plan ahead" eating plan that includes a balance of all the food groups in moderate portions
- **record your daily intentions for meals and snacks below**
- **review your progress and make daily adjustments**

breakfast

lunch

dinner

snacks

exercise regularly

- determine what type of activity, where, when, how often and with whom you most like to exercise
- develop a "week at a glance" exercise plan that includes a variety of 3 to 4 activities and has provision for alternate dates and times.

Detail your week plan; highlight today's plan.... what? when? where? with whom?

sun	mon	tue	wed	thur	fri	sat

journal

Journal below about any temptations, circumstances or emotions – today -- that might keep you from reaching your goals? (ex: vacation, celebrations, etc)

p
h
y
s
i
c
a
l

change
your
life
daily

date _____

forgive

To experience emotional balance on a daily basis, allow one or more of the below questions to prompt you to journal about the relationships in your life that need to heal and be healed.

Today, I know I need to ask _____ **to forgive me.**

I need to forgive myself for _____

I need to forgive _____ **for** _____

And I ask God to forgive me for _____

_____

_____

_____

_____

_____

_____

What additional step(s) can I take to complete the healing that I have just journaled about in the above space? (ex: a phone call, letter, apology, etc.)

_____

_____

_____

give

The gift of time, money, resources, or talent to an organization or person is both a powerful and practical way to help others.
What need comes to my mind -- today -- that I can find and fill and/or what person or organization needs a specific source of comfort or encouragement that I can give?

_____

_____

_____

_____

_____

date _____

talk to God

Today, in honest transparency, share -- in writing – your thoughts, gratitude, regrets, fears, plans, hopes, dreams and requests for yourself and others with the living, loving God.

s
p
i
r
i
t
u
a
l

_____

_____

_____

_____

_____

_____

_____

_____

_____

_____

_____

_____

_____

_____

_____

_____

_____

_____

_____

listen to God

God's voice is found in His word, the Bible.
Unless you have another system, read today's **change your life** Daily Bible
using Today's Date. Write in this area, any verse or verses that stand out,
touch your heart, encourage or correct you. **What is God saying to you today?**

_____

_____

_____

_____

_____

change
your
life
daily

date _____

m
e
n
t
a
l

detail your day

appointments

quiet time ☐
work out ☐
_____ ☐
_____ ☐
_____ ☐
_____ ☐
_____ ☐
_____ ☐
_____ ☐
_____ ☐
_____ ☐
_____ ☐
_____ ☐
_____ ☐
_____ ☐
_____ ☐
_____ ☐

calls to make   phone

_____
_____
_____
_____
_____

letters to write/fax/email
w f e
_____ ☐ ☐ ☐
_____ ☐ ☐ ☐
_____ ☐ ☐ ☐
_____ ☐ ☐ ☐

things to do

_____ ☐
_____ ☐
_____ ☐
_____ ☐
_____ ☐

define your dream

What is one practical step you can take toward reaching a goal -
and fulfilling a dream - in one or more areas of your life?
Use this space to brainstorm or to develop a dream that won't go away!

physical | emotional
mental | spiritual

change
your
life
daily

date _____

eat right

- · understand your own body type, genetics, metabolism, etc.
- · design a healthy, "plan ahead" eating plan that includes a balance of all the food groups in moderate portions
- · **record your daily intentions for meals and snacks below**
- · **review your progress and make daily adjustments**

breakfast _____

_____

lunch _____

_____

dinner _____

_____

snacks _____

exercise regularly

- · determine what type of activity, where, when, how often and with whom you most like to exercise
- · develop a "week at a glance" exercise plan that includes a variety of 3 to 4 activities and has provision for alternate dates and times.

Detail your week plan; highlight today's plan.... what? when? where? with whom?

sun	mon	tue	wed	thur	fri	sat

journal

Journal below about any temptations, circumstances or emotions – today -- that might keep you from reaching your goals? (ex: vacation, celebrations, etc)

_____

_____

_____

_____

_____

_____

p
h
y
s
i
c
a
l

change
your
life
daily

date _____

e
m
o
t
i
o
n
a
l

forgive

To experience emotional balance on a daily basis, allow one or more of the below questions to prompt you to journal about the relationships in your life that need to heal and be healed.

Today, I know I need to ask _____ **to forgive me.**

I need to forgive myself for _____

I need to forgive _____ **for** _____

And I ask God to forgive me for _____

_____

_____

_____

_____

_____

_____

What additional step(s) can I take to complete the healing that I have just journaled about in the above space? (ex: a phone call, letter, apology,etc.)

_____

_____

_____

_____

give

The gift of time, money, resources, or talent to an organization or person is both a powerful and practical way to help others.
What need comes to my mind -- today -- that I can find and fill and/or what person or organization needs a specific source of comfort or encouragement that I can give?

_____

_____

_____

_____

_____

_____

change
your
life
daily

date _____

talk to God

Today, in honest transparency, share -- in writing – your thoughts, gratitude, regrets, fears, plans, hopes, dreams and requests for yourself and others with the living, loving God.

s
p
i
r
i
t
u
a
l

_____

_____

_____

_____

_____

_____

_____

_____

_____

_____

_____

_____

_____

_____

_____

_____

_____

listen to God

God's voice is found in His word, the Bible.
Unless you have another system, read today's **change your life Daily Bible**
using Today's Date. Write in this area, any verse or verses that stand out,
touch your heart, encourage or correct you. **What is God saying to you today?**

_____

_____

_____

_____

_____

_____

change
your
life
daily

date _____

m
e
n
t
a
l

detail your day

appointments

quiet time	☐
work out	☐
	☐
	☐
	☐
	☐
	☐
	☐
	☐
	☐
	☐
	☐
	☐
	☐
	☐
	☐
	☐
	☐
	☐

calls to make   *phone #*

letters to write/fax/email
w   f   e
☐ ☐ ☐
☐ ☐ ☐
☐ ☐ ☐
☐ ☐ ☐

things to do

☐
☐
☐
☐
☐

define your dream

What is one practical step you can take toward reaching a goal -
and fulfilling a dream - in one or more areas of your life?
Use this space to brainstorm or to develop a dream that won't go away!

physical | emotional
mental | spiritual

change
your
life
daily

date _____

eat right

- understand your own body type, genetics, metabolism, etc.
- design a healthy, "plan ahead" eating plan that includes a balance of all the food groups in moderate portions
- **record your daily intentions for meals and snacks below**
- **review your progress and make daily adjustments**

p
h
y
s
i
c
a
l

breakfast

lunch

dinner

snacks

exercise regularly

- determine what type of activity, where, when, how often and with whom you most like to exercise
- develop a "week at a glance" exercise plan that includes a variety of 3 to 4 activities and has provision for alternate dates and times.

Detail your week plan; highlight today's plan.... what? when? where? with whom?

sun	mon	tue	wed	thur	fri	sat

journal

Journal below about any temptations, circumstances or emotions – today -- that might keep you from reaching your goals? (ex: vacation, celebrations, etc)

change
your
life
daily

date _____

e

m

o

t

i

o

n

a

l

forgive

To experience emotional balance on a daily basis, allow one or more of the below questions to prompt you to journal about the relationships in your life that need to heal and be healed.

Today, I know I need to ask _____ **to forgive me.**

I need to forgive myself for _____

I need to forgive _____ **for** _____

And I ask God to forgive me for _____

_____

_____

_____

_____

_____

_____

What additional step(s) can I take to complete the healing that I have just journaled about in the above space? (ex: a phone call, letter, apology, etc.)

_____

_____

_____

_____

give

The gift of time, money, resources, or talent to an organization or person is both a powerful and practical way to help others.
What need comes to my mind -- today -- that I can find and fill and/or what person or organization needs a specific source of comfort or encouragement that I can give?

_____

_____

_____

_____

_____

_____

change

your

life

daily

date _____

talk to God

Today, in honest transparency, share -- in writing – your thoughts,
gratitude, regrets, fears, plans, hopes, dreams and requests
for yourself and others with the living, loving God.

_____
_____
_____
_____
_____
_____
_____
_____
_____
_____
_____
_____
_____
_____
_____
_____
_____

s
p
i
r
i
t
u
a
l

listen to God

God's voice is found in His word, the Bible.
Unless you have another system, read today's **change your life** Daily Bible
using Today's Date. Write in this area, any verse or verses that stand out,
touch your heart, encourage or correct you. **What is God saying to you today?**

_____
_____
_____
_____
_____
_____

change
your
life
daily

date _____

m
e
n
t
a
l

detail your day

appointments

quiet time	☐
work out	☐
	☐
	☐
	☐
	☐
	☐
	☐
	☐
	☐
	☐
	☐
	☐
	☐
	☐
	☐
	☐

calls to make   *phone #*

letters to write/fax/email
w   f   e
☐ ☐ ☐
☐ ☐ ☐
☐ ☐ ☐
☐ ☐ ☐

things to do

☐
☐
☐
☐
☐

define your dream

What is one practical step you can take toward reaching a goal -
and fulfilling a dream - in one or more areas of your life?
Use this space to brainstorm or to develop a dream that won't go away!

physical | emotional
mental | spiritual

change

your

life

daily

date _____

eat right

- · understand your own body type, genetics, metabolism, etc.
- · design a healthy, "plan ahead" eating plan that includes a balance of all the food groups in moderate portions
- · **record your daily intentions for meals and snacks below**
- · **review your progress and make daily adjustments**

p
h
y
s
i
c
a
l

breakfast _____

_____

lunch _____

_____

dinner _____

_____

snacks _____

exercise regularly

- · determine what type of activity, where, when, how often and with whom you most like to exercise
- · develop a "week at a glance" exercise plan that includes a variety of 3 to 4 activities and has provision for alternate dates and times.

Detail your week plan; highlight today's plan.... what? when? where? with whom?

sun	mon	tue	wed	thur	fri	sat

journal

Journal below about any temptations, circumstances or emotions – today -- that might keep you from reaching your goals? (ex: vacation, celebrations, etc)

_____

_____

_____

_____

_____

_____

change
your
life
daily

date _____

e
m
o
t
i
o
n
a
l

forgive

To experience emotional balance on a daily basis, allow one or more of the below questions to prompt you to journal about the relationships in your life that need to heal and be healed.

Today, I know I need to ask _____ **to forgive me.**

I need to forgive myself for _____

I need to forgive _____ **for** _____

And I ask God to forgive me for _____

_____

_____

_____

_____

_____

_____

What additional step(s) can I take to complete the healing that I have just journaled about in the above space? (ex: a phone call, letter, apology,etc.)

_____

_____

_____

_____

give

The gift of time, money, resources, or talent to an organization or person is both a powerful and practical way to help others.
What need comes to my mind -- today -- that I can find and fill and/or what person or organization needs a specific source of comfort or encouragement that I can give?

_____

_____

_____

_____

_____

change
your
life
daily

date _____

talk to God

Today, in honest transparency, share -- in writing – your thoughts, gratitude, regrets, fears, plans, hopes, dreams and requests for yourself and others with the living, loving God.

s
p
i
r
i
t
u
a
l

_____

_____

_____

_____

_____

_____

_____

_____

_____

_____

_____

_____

_____

_____

_____

_____

_____

listen to God

God's voice is found in His word, the Bible.
Unless you have another system, read today's **change your life** **Daily Bible** using Today's Date. Write in this area, any verse or verses that stand out, touch your heart, encourage or correct you. **What is God saying to you today?**

_____

_____

_____

_____

_____

_____

change
your
life
daily

date _____

m
e
n
t
a
l

detail your day

appointments
quiet time ☐
work out ☐
_____ ☐
_____ ☐
_____ ☐
_____ ☐
_____ ☐
_____ ☐
_____ ☐
_____ ☐
_____ ☐
_____ ☐
_____ ☐
_____ ☐
_____ ☐
_____ ☐
_____ ☐

calls to make   *phone #*
_____
_____
_____
_____

letters to write/fax/email
w f e
_____ ☐ ☐ ☐
_____ ☐ ☐ ☐
_____ ☐ ☐ ☐
_____ ☐ ☐ ☐

things to do
_____ ☐
_____ ☐
_____ ☐
_____ ☐
_____ ☐

define your dream
What is one practical step you can take toward reaching a goal -
and fulfilling a dream - in one or more areas of your life?
Use this space to brainstorm or to develop a dream that won't go away!

physical | emotional
mental | spiritual

change
your
life
daily

date _____

eat right

- · understand your own body type, genetics, metabolism, etc.
- · design a healthy, "plan ahead" eating plan that includes a balance of all the food groups in moderate portions
- · **record your daily intentions for meals and snacks below**
- · **review your progress and make daily adjustments**

breakfast	
lunch	
dinner	
snacks	

exercise regularly

- · determine what type of activity, where, when, how often and with whom you most like to exercise
- · develop a "week at a glance" exercise plan that includes a variety of 3 to 4 activities and has provision for alternate dates and times.

Detail your week plan; highlight today's plan.... what? when? where? with whom?

sun	mon	tue	wed	thur	fri	sat

journal

Journal below about any temptations, circumstances or emotions – today -- that might keep you from reaching your goals? (ex: vacation, celebrations, etc)

_____

_____

_____

_____

_____

_____

p
h
y
s
i
c
a
l

change
your
life
daily

date _____

e
m
o
t
i
o
n
a
l

forgive

To experience emotional balance on a daily basis, allow one or more of the below questions to prompt you to journal about the relationships in your life that need to heal and be healed.

Today, I know I need to ask _____ **to forgive me.**

I need to forgive myself for _____

I need to forgive _____ **for** _____

And I ask God to forgive me for _____

_____

_____

_____

_____

_____

_____

What additional step(s) can I take to complete the healing that I have just journaled about in the above space? (ex: a phone call, letter, apology,etc.)

_____

_____

_____

_____

give

The gift of time, money, resources, or talent to an organization or person is both a powerful and practical way to help others.
What need comes to my mind -- today -- that I can find and fill and/or what person or organization needs a specific source of comfort or encouragement that I can give?

_____

_____

_____

_____

_____

change
your
life
daily

date _____

talk to God

Today, in honest transparency, share -- in writing – your thoughts,
gratitude, regrets, fears, plans, hopes, dreams and requests
for yourself and others with the living, loving God.

s
p
i
r
i
t
u
a
l

_____
_____
_____
_____
_____
_____
_____
_____
_____
_____
_____
_____
_____
_____
_____
_____
_____

listen to God

God's voice is found in His word, the Bible.
Unless you have another system, read today's **change your life Daily Bible**
using Today's Date. Write in this area, any verse or verses that stand out,
touch your heart, encourage or correct you. **What is God saying to you today?**

_____
_____
_____
_____
_____
_____

change
your
life
daily

date _____

m
e
n
t
a
l

detail your day

appointments

quiet time ☐
work out ☐
☐
☐
☐
☐
☐
☐
☐
☐
☐
☐
☐
☐
☐
☐

calls to make   *phone #*

_____
_____
_____
_____
_____

letters to write/fax/email
                    w   f   e
_____ ☐ ☐ ☐
_____ ☐ ☐ ☐
_____ ☐ ☐ ☐
_____ ☐ ☐ ☐

things to do

_____ ☐
_____ ☐
_____ ☐
_____ ☐
_____ ☐

define your dream

What is one practical step you can take toward reaching a goal -
and fulfilling a dream - in one or more areas of your life?
Use this space to brainstorm or to develop a dream that won't go away!

physical | emotional
mental | spiritual

change
your
life
daily

date _____

eat right

- · understand your own body type, genetics, metabolism, etc.
- · design a healthy, "plan ahead" eating plan that includes a balance of all the food groups in moderate portions
- · **record your daily intentions for meals and snacks below**
- · **review your progress and make daily adjustments**

p
h
y
s
i
c
a
l

breakfast

lunch

dinner

snacks

exercise regularly

- · determine what type of activity, where, when, how often and with whom you most like to exercise
- · develop a "week at a glance" exercise plan that includes a variety of 3 to 4 activities and has provision for alternate dates and times.

Detail your week plan; highlight today's plan.... what? when? where? with whom?

sun	mon	tue	wed	thur	fri	sat

journal

Journal below about any temptations, circumstances or emotions – today -- that might keep you from reaching your goals? (ex: vacation, celebrations, etc)

change
your
life
daily

date _____

e
m
o
t
i
o
n
a
l

forgive

To experience emotional balance on a daily basis, allow one or more of the below questions to prompt you to journal about the relationships in your life that need to heal and be healed.

Today, I know I need to ask _____ **to forgive me.**

I need to forgive myself for _____

I need to forgive _____ **for** _____

And I ask God to forgive me for _____

_____

_____

_____

_____

_____

_____

What additional step(s) can I take to complete the healing that I have just journaled about in the above space? (ex: a phone call, letter, apology,etc.)

_____

_____

_____

_____

give

The gift of time, money, resources, or talent to an organization or person is both a powerful and practical way to help others.
What need comes to my mind -- today -- that I can find and fill and/or what person or organization needs a specific source of comfort or encouragement that I can give?

_____

_____

_____

_____

_____

change
your
life
daily

date _____

talk to God

Today, in honest transparency, share -- in writing – your thoughts, gratitude, regrets, fears, plans, hopes, dreams and requests for yourself and others with the living, loving God.

s
p
i
r
i
t
u
a
l

_____
_____
_____
_____
_____
_____
_____
_____
_____
_____
_____
_____
_____
_____
_____
_____
_____
_____
_____

listen to God

God's voice is found in His word, the Bible.
Unless you have another system, read today's **change your life** **Daily Bible** using Today's Date. Write in this area, any verse or verses that stand out, touch your heart, encourage or correct you. **What is God saying to you today?**

_____
_____
_____
_____
_____
_____

change
your
life
daily

date _____

m
e
n
t
a
l

detail your day

appointments

- quiet time ☐
- work out ☐
- ☐
- ☐
- ☐
- ☐
- ☐
- ☐
- ☐
- ☐
- ☐
- ☐
- ☐
- ☐
- ☐
- ☐
- ☐

calls to make   *phone #*

_____
_____
_____
_____
_____

letters to write/fax/email
                              w   f   e
_____ ☐ ☐ ☐
_____ ☐ ☐ ☐
_____ ☐ ☐ ☐
_____ ☐ ☐ ☐

things to do

_____ ☐
_____ ☐
_____ ☐
_____ ☐
_____ ☐

define your dream

What is one practical step you can take toward reaching a goal -
and fulfilling a dream - in one or more areas of your life?
Use this space to brainstorm or to develop a dream that won't go away!

physical | emotional

mental | spiritual

change

your

life

daily

date _____

eat right

- · understand your own body type, genetics, metabolism, etc.
- · design a healthy, "plan ahead" eating plan that includes a balance of all the food groups in moderate portions
- · **record your daily intentions for meals and snacks below**
- · **review your progress and make daily adjustments**

breakfast |
lunch |
dinner |
snacks |

p
h
y
s
i
c
a
l

exercise regularly

- · determine what type of activity, where, when, how often and with whom you most like to exercise
- · develop a "week at a glance" exercise plan that includes a variety of 3 to 4 activities and has provision for alternate dates and times.

Detail your week plan; highlight today's plan.... what? when? where? with whom?

sun	mon	tue	wed	thur	fri	sat

journal

Journal below about any temptations, circumstances or emotions – today -- that might keep you from reaching your goals? (ex: vacation, celebrations, etc)

change
your
life
daily

date _____

e
m
o
t
i
o
n
a
l

forgive

To experience emotional balance on a daily basis, allow one or more of the below questions to prompt you to journal about the relationships in your life that need to heal and be healed.

Today, I know I need to ask _____ **to forgive me.**

I need to forgive myself for _____

I need to forgive _____ **for** _____

And I ask God to forgive me for _____

_____

_____

_____

_____

_____

_____

What additional step(s) can I take to complete the healing that I have just journaled about in the above space? (ex: a phone call, letter, apology,etc.)

_____

_____

_____

give

The gift of time, money, resources, or talent to an organization or person is both a powerful and practical way to help others.
What need comes to my mind -- today -- that I can find and fill and/or what person or organization needs a specific source of comfort or encouragement that I can give?

_____

_____

_____

_____

_____

change
your
life
daily

date _____

talk to God

Today, in honest transparency, share -- in writing – your thoughts,
gratitude, regrets, fears, plans, hopes, dreams and requests
for yourself and others with the living, loving God.

s
p
i
r
i
t
u
a
l

_____

_____

_____

_____

_____

_____

_____

_____

_____

_____

_____

_____

_____

_____

_____

_____

_____

_____

_____

listen to God

God's voice is found in His word, the Bible.
Unless you have another system, read today's **change your life** Daily Bible
using Today's Date. Write in this area, any verse or verses that stand out,
touch your heart, encourage or correct you. **What is God saying to you today?**

_____

_____

_____

_____

_____

_____

change
your
life
daily

date _____

m
e
n
t
a
l

detail your day

appointments

quiet time ☐
work out ☐
_____ ☐
_____ ☐
_____ ☐
_____ ☐
_____ ☐
_____ ☐
_____ ☐
_____ ☐
_____ ☐
_____ ☐
_____ ☐
_____ ☐
_____ ☐
_____ ☐
_____ ☐

calls to make   *phone #*

_____
_____
_____
_____
_____

letters to write/fax/email
        w   f   e
_____ ☐ ☐ ☐
_____ ☐ ☐ ☐
_____ ☐ ☐ ☐
_____ ☐ ☐ ☐

things to do

_____ ☐
_____ ☐
_____ ☐
_____ ☐
_____ ☐

define your dream

What is one practical step you can take toward reaching a goal -
and fulfilling a dream - in one or more areas of your life?
Use this space to brainstorm or to develop a dream that won't go away!

physical | emotional
mental | spiritual

change
your
life
daily

date _____

eat right

- · understand your own body type, genetics, metabolism, etc.
- · design a healthy, "plan ahead" eating plan that includes a balance
    of all the food groups in moderate portions
- · **record your daily intentions for meals and snacks below**
- · **review your progress and make daily adjustments**

breakfast _____

_____

lunch _____

_____

dinner _____

_____

snacks _____

p
h
y
s
i
c
a
l

exercise regularly

- · determine what type of activity, where, when, how often and with whom you
    most like to exercise
- · develop a "week at a glance" exercise plan that includes a variety of 3 to 4 activities
    and has provision for alternate dates and times.

Detail your week plan; highlight today's plan.... what? when? where? with whom?

sun	mon	tue	wed	thur	fri	sat

journal

**Journal below about any temptations, circumstances or emotions – today --
that might keep you from reaching your goals?** (ex: vacation, celebrations, etc)

_____

_____

_____

_____

_____

_____

change
your
life
daily

date _____

e
m
o
t
i
o
n
a
l

forgive

To experience emotional balance on a daily basis, allow one or more of the below questions to prompt you to journal about the relationships in your life that need to heal and be healed.

Today, I know I need to ask _____ **to forgive me.**

I need to forgive myself for _____

I need to forgive _____ **for** _____

And I ask God to forgive me for _____

_____

_____

_____

_____

_____

_____

What additional step(s) can I take to complete the healing that I have just journaled about in the above space? (ex: a phone call, letter, apology, etc.)

_____

_____

_____

_____

give

The gift of time, money, resources, or talent to an organization or person is both a powerful and practical way to help others.
What need comes to my mind -- today -- that I can find and fill and/or what person or organization needs a specific source of comfort or encouragement that I can give?

_____

_____

_____

_____

_____

change
your
life
daily

date _____

talk to God

Today, in honest transparency, share -- in writing – your thoughts, gratitude, regrets, fears, plans, hopes, dreams and requests for yourself and others with the living, loving God.

s
p
i
r
i
t
u
a
l

_____
_____
_____
_____
_____
_____
_____
_____
_____
_____
_____
_____
_____
_____
_____
_____
_____
_____
_____

listen to God

God's voice is found in His word, the Bible.
Unless you have another system, read today's **change your life Daily Bible** using Today's Date. Write in this area, any verse or verses that stand out, touch your heart, encourage or correct you. **What is God saying to you today?**

_____
_____
_____
_____
_____
_____

change
your
life
daily

date _____

m
e
n
t
a
l

detail your day

appointments

- *quiet time* ☐
- *work out* ☐
- ☐
- ☐
- ☐
- ☐
- ☐
- ☐
- ☐
- ☐
- ☐
- ☐
- ☐
- ☐
- ☐
- ☐
- ☐

calls to make   *phone #*

_____

_____

_____

_____

_____

letters to write/fax/email
                     w   f   e

_____ ☐ ☐ ☐

_____ ☐ ☐ ☐

_____ ☐ ☐ ☐

_____ ☐ ☐ ☐

things to do

_____ ☐

_____ ☐

_____ ☐

_____ ☐

_____ ☐

define your dream

What is one practical step you can take toward reaching a goal -
and fulfilling a dream - in one or more areas of your life?
Use this space to brainstorm or to develop a dream that won't go away!

physical | emotional

mental | spiritual

change

your

life

daily

date _____

eat right

- · understand your own body type, genetics, metabolism, etc.
- · design a healthy, "plan ahead" eating plan that includes a balance of all the food groups in moderate portions
- · **record your daily intentions for meals and snacks below**
- · **review your progress and make daily adjustments**

breakfast	
lunch	
dinner	
snacks	

p
h
y
s
i
c
a
l

exercise regularly

- · determine what type of activity, where, when, how often and with whom you most like to exercise
- · develop a "week at a glance" exercise plan that includes a variety of 3 to 4 activities and has provision for alternate dates and times.

Detail your week plan; highlight today's plan.... what? when? where? with whom?

sun	mon	tue	wed	thur	fri	sat

journal

Journal below about any temptations, circumstances or emotions – today -- that might keep you from reaching your goals? (ex: vacation, celebrations, etc)

_____

_____

_____

_____

_____

change
your
life
daily

date _____

e
m
o
t
i
o
n
a
l

forgive

To experience emotional balance on a daily basis, allow one or more of the below questions to prompt you to journal about the relationships in your life that need to heal and be healed.

Today, I know I need to ask _____ **to forgive me.**

I need to forgive myself for _____

I need to forgive _____ **for** _____

And I ask God to forgive me for _____

_____

_____

_____

_____

_____

_____

What additional step(s) can I take to complete the healing that I have just journaled about in the above space? (ex: a phone call, letter, apology,etc.)

_____

_____

_____

_____

give

The gift of time, money, resources, or talent to an organization or person is both a powerful and practical way to help others.
What need comes to my mind -- today -- that I can find and fill and/or what person or organization needs a specific source of comfort or encouragement that I can give?

_____

_____

_____

_____

_____

change

your

life

daily

date _____

talk to God

Today, in honest transparency, share -- in writing – your thoughts, gratitude, regrets, fears, plans, hopes, dreams and requests for yourself and others with the living, loving God.

s
p
i
r
i
t
u
a
l

listen to God

God's voice is found in His word, the Bible.
Unless you have another system, read today's **change your life Daily Bible**
using Today's Date. Write in this area, any verse or verses that stand out,
touch your heart, encourage or correct you. **What is God saying to you today?**

change
your
life
daily

date _____

m
e
n
t
a
l

detail your day

appointments

quiet time ☐
work out ☐
_____ ☐
_____ ☐
_____ ☐
_____ ☐
_____ ☐
_____ ☐
_____ ☐
_____ ☐
_____ ☐
_____ ☐
_____ ☐
_____ ☐
_____ ☐
_____ ☐
_____ ☐

calls to make   _phone #_

_____
_____
_____
_____
_____

letters to write/fax/email
_w   f   e_
☐ ☐ ☐
☐ ☐ ☐
☐ ☐ ☐
☐ ☐ ☐

things to do

_____ ☐
_____ ☐
_____ ☐
_____ ☐
_____ ☐

define your dream

What is one practical step you can take toward reaching a goal -
and fulfilling a dream - in one or more areas of your life?
Use this space to brainstorm or to develop a dream that won't go away!

physical | emotional
mental | spiritual

change
your
life
daily

date _____

eat right

- · understand your own body type, genetics, metabolism, etc.
- · design a healthy, "plan ahead" eating plan that includes a balance of all the food groups in moderate portions
- · **record your daily intentions for meals and snacks below**
- · **review your progress and make daily adjustments**

breakfast	
lunch	
dinner	
snacks	

exercise regularly

- · determine what type of activity, where, when, how often and with whom you most like to exercise
- · develop a "week at a glance" exercise plan that includes a variety of 3 to 4 activities and has provision for alternate dates and times.

Detail your week plan; highlight today's plan ... what? when? where? with whom?

sun	mon	tue	wed	thur	fri	sat

journal

Journal below about any temptations, circumstances or emotions – today -- that might keep you from reaching your goals? (ex: vacation, celebrations, etc)

_____

_____

_____

_____

_____

_____

physical

change your life daily

date _____

e

m

o

t

i

o

n

a

l

forgive

To experience emotional balance on a daily basis, allow one or more of the below questions to prompt you to journal about the relationships in your life that need to heal and be healed.

Today, I know I need to ask _____ **to forgive me.**

I need to forgive myself for _____

I need to forgive _____ **for** _____

And I ask God to forgive me for _____

_____

_____

_____

_____

_____

_____

What additional step(s) can I take to complete the healing that I have just journaled about in the above space? (ex: a phone call, letter, apology,etc.)

_____

_____

_____

give

The gift of time, money, resources, or talent to an organization or person is both a powerful and practical way to help others.
What need comes to my mind -- today -- that I can find and fill and/or what person or organization needs a specific source of comfort or encouragement that I can give?

_____

_____

_____

_____

_____

change

your

life

daily

date _____

talk to God

Today, in honest transparency, share -- in writing – your thoughts, gratitude, regrets, fears, plans, hopes, dreams and requests for yourself and others with the living, loving God.

s
p
i
r
i
t
u
a
l

_____
_____
_____
_____
_____
_____
_____
_____
_____
_____
_____
_____
_____
_____
_____
_____
_____
_____

listen to God

God's voice is found in His word, the Bible.
Unless you have another system, read today's **change your life Daily Bible** using Today's Date. Write in this area, any verse or verses that stand out, touch your heart, encourage or correct you. **What is God saying to you today?**

_____
_____
_____
_____
_____
_____

change
your
life
daily

date _____

m
e
n
t
a
l

detail your day

appointments

- *quiet time* ☐
- *work out* ☐
- _____ ☐
- _____ ☐
- _____ ☐
- _____ ☐
- _____ ☐
- _____ ☐
- _____ ☐
- _____ ☐
- _____ ☐
- _____ ☐
- _____ ☐
- _____ ☐
- _____ ☐
- _____ ☐
- _____ ☐

calls to make   *phone #*

- _____
- _____
- _____
- _____
- _____

letters to write/fax/email
w   f   e

- _____ ☐ ☐ ☐
- _____ ☐ ☐ ☐
- _____ ☐ ☐ ☐
- _____ ☐ ☐ ☐

things to do

- _____ ☐
- _____ ☐
- _____ ☐
- _____ ☐
- _____ ☐

define your dream

What is one practical step you can take toward reaching a goal -
and fulfilling a dream - in one or more areas of your life?
Use this space to brainstorm or to develop a dream that won't go away!

physical | emotional
mental | spiritual

change
your
life
daily

date _____

eat right

- · understand your own body type, genetics, metabolism, etc.
- · design a healthy, "plan ahead" eating plan that includes a balance of all the food groups in moderate portions
- · **record your daily intentions for meals and snacks below**
- · **review your progress and make daily adjustments**

breakfast	
lunch	
dinner	
snacks	

exercise regularly

- · determine what type of activity, where, when, how often and with whom you most like to exercise
- · develop a "week at a glance" exercise plan that includes a variety of 3 to 4 activities and has provision for alternate dates and times.

Detail your week plan; highlight today's plan.... what? when? where? with whom?

sun	mon	tue	wed	thur	fri	sat

journal

Journal below about any temptations, circumstances or emotions – today -- that might keep you from reaching your goals? (ex: vacation, celebrations, etc)

_____

_____

_____

_____

_____

_____

p
h
y
s
i
c
a
l

change
your
life
daily

date _____

e
m
o
t
i
o
n
a
l

forgive

To experience emotional balance on a daily basis, allow one or more of the below questions to prompt you to journal about the relationships in your life that need to heal and be healed.

Today, I know I need to ask _____ **to forgive me.**

I need to forgive myself for _____

I need to forgive _____ **for** _____

And I ask God to forgive me for _____

_____

_____

_____

_____

_____

_____

What additional step(s) can I take to complete the healing that I have just journaled about in the above space? (ex: a phone call, letter, apology, etc.)

_____

_____

_____

give

The gift of time, money, resources, or talent to an organization or person is both a powerful and practical way to help others.
What need comes to my mind -- today -- that I can find and fill and/or what person or organization needs a specific source of comfort or encouragement that I can give?

_____

_____

_____

_____

_____

change
your
life
daily

talk to God

Today, in honest transparency, share -- in writing – your thoughts,
gratitude, regrets, fears, plans, hopes, dreams and requests
for yourself and others with the living, loving God.

s
p
i
r
i
t
u
a
l

_____
_____
_____
_____
_____
_____
_____
_____
_____
_____
_____
_____
_____
_____
_____
_____
_____

listen to God

God's voice is found in His word, the Bible.
Unless you have another system, read today's **change your life Daily Bible**
using Today's Date. Write in this area, any verse or verses that stand out,
touch your heart, encourage or correct you. **What is God saying to you today?**

_____
_____
_____
_____
_____
_____

change
your
life
daily

date _____

m
e
n
t
a
l

detail your day

appointments ☐

quiet time ☐
work out ☐
_____ ☐
_____ ☐
_____ ☐
_____ ☐
_____ ☐
_____ ☐
_____ ☐
_____ ☐
_____ ☐
_____ ☐
_____ ☐
_____ ☐
_____ ☐
_____ ☐
_____ ☐

calls to make   *phone #*

_____
_____
_____
_____
_____

letters to write/fax/email
w   f   e
_____ ☐ ☐ ☐
_____ ☐ ☐ ☐
_____ ☐ ☐ ☐
_____ ☐ ☐ ☐

things to do

_____ ☐
_____ ☐
_____ ☐
_____ ☐
_____ ☐

define your dream

What is one practical step you can take toward reaching a goal -
and fulfilling a dream - in one or more areas of your life?
Use this space to brainstorm or to develop a dream that won't go away!

physical | emotional
mental | spiritual

change
your
life
daily

date _____

eat right

- understand your own body type, genetics, metabolism, etc.
- design a healthy, "plan ahead" eating plan that includes a balance of all the food groups in moderate portions
- **record your daily intentions for meals and snacks below**
- **review your progress and make daily adjustments**

breakfast	
lunch	
dinner	
snacks	

exercise regularly

- determine what type of activity, where, when, how often and with whom you most like to exercise
- develop a "week at a glance" exercise plan that includes a variety of 3 to 4 activities and has provision for alternate dates and times.

Detail your week plan; highlight today's plan.... what? when? where? with whom?

sun	mon	tue	wed	thur	fri	sat

journal

Journal below about any temptations, circumstances or emotions – today -- that might keep you from reaching your goals? (ex: vacation, celebrations, etc)

_____

_____

_____

_____

_____

_____

p
h
y
s
i
c
a
l

change
your
life
daily

date _____

e
m
o
t
i
o
n
a
l

forgive

To experience emotional balance on a daily basis, allow one or more of the below questions to prompt you to journal about the relationships in your life that need to heal and be healed.

Today, I know I need to ask _____ **to forgive me.**

I need to forgive myself for _____

I need to forgive _____ **for** _____

And I ask God to forgive me for _____

_____

_____

_____

_____

_____

_____

What additional step(s) can I take to complete the healing that I have just journaled about in the above space? (ex: a phone call, letter, apology,etc.)

_____

_____

_____

_____

give

The gift of time, money, resources, or talent to an organization or person is both a powerful and practical way to help others.
What need comes to my mind -- today -- that I can find and fill and/or what person or organization needs a specific source of comfort or encouragement that I can give?

_____

_____

_____

_____

_____

change
your
life
daily

date _____

talk to God

Today, in honest transparency, share -- in writing – your thoughts, gratitude, regrets, fears, plans, hopes, dreams and requests for yourself and others with the living, loving God.

s
p
i
r
i
t
u
a
l

_____
_____
_____
_____
_____
_____
_____
_____
_____
_____
_____
_____
_____
_____
_____
_____
_____
_____
_____
_____
_____
_____

listen to God

God's voice is found in His word, the Bible.
Unless you have another system, read today's **change your life Daily Bible** using Today's Date. Write in this area, any verse or verses that stand out, touch your heart, encourage or correct you. **What is God saying to you today?**

_____
_____
_____
_____
_____
_____

change
your
life
daily

date _____

m
e
n
t
a
l

detail your day

appointments

quiet time ☐

work out ☐

_____ ☐
_____ ☐
_____ ☐
_____ ☐
_____ ☐
_____ ☐
_____ ☐
_____ ☐
_____ ☐
_____ ☐
_____ ☐
_____ ☐
_____ ☐
_____ ☐
_____ ☐
_____ ☐

calls to make   *phone #*

_____
_____
_____
_____
_____

letters to write/fax/email
                               w   f   e
_____   ☐ ☐ ☐
_____   ☐ ☐ ☐
_____   ☐ ☐ ☐
_____   ☐ ☐ ☐

things to do

_____   ☐
_____   ☐
_____   ☐
_____   ☐
_____   ☐

define your dream

What is one practical step you can take toward reaching a goal -
and fulfilling a dream - in one or more areas of your life?
Use this space to brainstorm or to develop a dream that won't go away!

physical | emotional
mental | spiritual

change
your
life
daily

date _____

eat right

- · understand your own body type, genetics, metabolism, etc.
- · design a healthy, "plan ahead" eating plan that includes a balance of all the food groups in moderate portions
- · **record your daily intentions for meals and snacks below**
- · **review your progress and make daily adjustments**

breakfast	
lunch	
dinner	
snacks	

exercise regularly

- · determine what type of activity, where, when, how often and with whom you most like to exercise
- · develop a "week at a glance" exercise plan that includes a variety of 3 to 4 activities and has provision for alternate dates and times.

Detail your week plan; highlight today's plan.... what? when? where? with whom?

sun	mon	tue	wed	thur	fri	sat

journal

Journal below about any temptations, circumstances or emotions – today -- that might keep you from reaching your goals? (ex: vacation, celebrations, etc)

_____

_____

_____

_____

_____

p
h
y
s
i
c
a
l

change
your
life
daily

date _____

e
m
o
t
i
o
n
a
l

forgive

To experience emotional balance on a daily basis, allow one or more of the below questions to prompt you to journal about the relationships in your life that need to heal and be healed.

Today, I know I need to ask _____ **to forgive me.**

I need to forgive myself for _____

I need to forgive _____ **for** _____

And I ask God to forgive me for _____

_____

_____

_____

_____

_____

_____

What additional step(s) can I take to complete the healing that I have just journaled about in the above space? (ex: a phone call, letter, apology,etc.)

_____

_____

_____

_____

give

The gift of time, money, resources, or talent to an organization or person is both a powerful and practical way to help others.
What need comes to my mind -- today -- that I can find and fill and/or what person or organization needs a specific source of comfort or encouragement that I can give?

_____

_____

_____

_____

_____

change
your
life
daily

date _____

talk to God

Today, in honest transparency, share -- in writing – your thoughts, gratitude, regrets, fears, plans, hopes, dreams and requests for yourself and others with the living, loving God.

s
p
i
r
i
t
u
a
l

listen to God

God's voice is found in His word, the Bible.
Unless you have another system, read today's **change your life** **Daily Bible** using Today's Date. Write in this area, any verse or verses that stand out, touch your heart, encourage or correct you. **What is God saying to you today?**

change
your
life
daily

date _____

m
e
n
t
a
l

detail your day

appointments

quiet time	☐
work out	☐
	☐
	☐
	☐
	☐
	☐
	☐
	☐
	☐
	☐
	☐
	☐
	☐
	☐
	☐
	☐

calls to make   *phone #*

letters to write/fax/email
w   f   e
☐ ☐ ☐
☐ ☐ ☐
☐ ☐ ☐
☐ ☐ ☐

things to do
☐
☐
☐
☐
☐

define your dream

What is one practical step you can take toward reaching a goal -
and fulfilling a dream - in one or more areas of your life?
Use this space to brainstorm or to develop a dream that won't go away!

physical	emotional
mental	spiritual

change
your
life
daily

date _____

eat right

- understand your own body type, genetics, metabolism, etc.
- design a healthy, "plan ahead" eating plan that includes a balance of all the food groups in moderate portions
- **record your daily intentions for meals and snacks below**
- **review your progress and make daily adjustments**

breakfast	
lunch	
dinner	
snacks	

exercise regularly

- determine what type of activity, where, when, how often and with whom you most like to exercise
- develop a "week at a glance" exercise plan that includes a variety of 3 to 4 activities and has provision for alternate dates and times.

Detail your week plan; highlight today's plan.... what? when? where? with whom?

sun	mon	tue	wed	thur	fri	sat

journal

Journal below about any temptations, circumstances or emotions – today -- that might keep you from reaching your goals? (ex: vacation, celebrations, etc)

_____

_____

_____

_____

_____

_____

p
h
y
s
i
c
a
l

change
your
life
daily

date _____

forgive

To experience emotional balance on a daily basis, allow one or more of the below questions to prompt you to journal about the relationships in your life that need to heal and be healed.

Today, I know I need to ask _____ **to forgive me.**

I need to forgive myself for _____

I need to forgive _____ **for** _____

And I ask God to forgive me for _____

_____

_____

_____

_____

_____

_____

What additional step(s) can I take to complete the healing that I have just journaled about in the above space? (ex: a phone call, letter, apology,etc.)

_____

_____

_____

_____

give

The gift of time, money, resources, or talent to an organization or person is both a powerful and practical way to help others.
What need comes to my mind -- today -- that I can find and fill and/or what person or organization needs a specific source of comfort or encouragement that I can give?

_____

_____

_____

_____

_____

_____

date _____

talk to God

Today, in honest transparency, share -- in writing – your thoughts,
gratitude, regrets, fears, plans, hopes, dreams and requests
for yourself and others with the living, loving God.

s
p
i
r
i
t
u
a
l

_____

_____

_____

_____

_____

_____

_____

_____

_____

_____

_____

_____

_____

_____

_____

_____

_____

_____

listen to God

God's voice is found in His word, the Bible.
Unless you have another system, read today's **change your life Daily Bible**
using Today's Date. Write in this area, any verse or verses that stand out,
touch your heart, encourage or correct you. **What is God saying to you today?**

_____

_____

_____

_____

_____

change
your
life
daily

date _____

detail your day

appointments

quiet time ☐
work out ☐
☐
☐
☐
☐
☐
☐
☐
☐
☐
☐
☐
☐
☐
☐
☐

calls to make *phone #*

_____
_____
_____
_____
_____
_____

letters to write/fax/email
w   f   e
☐ ☐ ☐
☐ ☐ ☐
☐ ☐ ☐
☐ ☐ ☐

things to do

☐
☐
☐
☐
☐

define your dream

What is one practical step you can take toward reaching a goal -
and fulfilling a dream - in one or more areas of your life?

Use this space to brainstorm or to develop a dream that won't go away!

physical | emotional

mental | spiritual

change
your
life
daily

date _____

eat right

- understand your own body type, genetics, metabolism, etc.
- design a healthy, "plan ahead" eating plan that includes a balance of all the food groups in moderate portions
- **record your daily intentions for meals and snacks below**
- **review your progress and make daily adjustments**

breakfast	_____
	_____
lunch	_____
	_____
dinner	_____
	_____
snacks	_____

exercise regularly

- determine what type of activity, where, when, how often and with whom you most like to exercise
- develop a "week at a glance" exercise plan that includes a variety of 3 to 4 activities and has provision for alternate dates and times.

Detail your week plan; highlight today's plan.... what? when? where? with whom?

sun	mon	tue	wed	thur	fri	sat

journal

Journal below about any temptations, circumstances or emotions – today -- that might keep you from reaching your goals? (ex: vacation, celebrations, etc)

_____

_____

_____

_____

_____

_____

p
h
y
s
i
c
a
l

change
your
life
daily

date _____

e

m

o

t

i

o

n

a

l

forgive

To experience emotional balance on a daily basis, allow one or more of the below questions to prompt you to journal about the relationships in your life that need to heal and be healed.

Today, I know I need to ask _____ **to forgive me.**

I need to forgive myself for _____

I need to forgive _____ **for** _____

And I ask God to forgive me for _____

_____

_____

_____

_____

_____

_____

_____

What additional step(s) can I take to complete the healing that I have just journaled about in the above space? (ex: a phone call, letter, apology,etc.)

_____

_____

_____

_____

give

The gift of time, money, resources, or talent to an organization or person is both a powerful and practical way to help others.
What need comes to my mind -- today -- that I can find and fill and/or what person or organization needs a specific source of comfort or encouragement that I can give?

_____

_____

_____

_____

_____

change

your

life

daily

date _____

talk to God

Today, in honest transparency, share -- in writing – your thoughts, gratitude, regrets, fears, plans, hopes, dreams and requests for yourself and others with the living, loving God.

s
p
i
r
i
t
u
a
l

_____

_____

_____

_____

_____

_____

_____

_____

_____

_____

_____

_____

_____

_____

_____

_____

_____

_____

listen to God

God's voice is found in His word, the Bible.
Unless you have another system, read today's **change your life** Daily Bible using Today's Date. Write in this area, any verse or verses that stand out, touch your heart, encourage or correct you. **What is God saying to you today?**

_____

_____

_____

_____

_____

_____

change
your
life
daily

date _____

m

e

n

t

a

l

detail your day

appointments

quiet time	☐
work out	☐
	☐
	☐
	☐
	☐
	☐
	☐
	☐
	☐
	☐
	☐
	☐
	☐
	☐
	☐
	☐

calls to make   phone

_____

_____

_____

_____

_____

letters to write/fax/email
w   f   e
☐ ☐ ☐

☐ ☐ ☐

☐ ☐ ☐

☐ ☐ ☐

things to do

	☐
	☐
	☐
	☐
	☐

define your dream

What is one practical step you can take toward reaching a goal -
and fulfilling a dream - in one or more areas of your life?
Use this space to brainstorm or to develop a dream that won't go away!

physical | emotional

mental | spiritual

change

your

life

daily

date _____

eat right

- · understand your own body type, genetics, metabolism, etc.
- · design a healthy, "plan ahead" eating plan that includes a balance of all the food groups in moderate portions
- · **record your daily intentions for meals and snacks below**
- · **review your progress and make daily adjustments**

breakfast _____

_____

lunch _____

_____

dinner _____

_____

snacks _____

p
h
y
s
i
c
a
l

exercise regularly

- · determine what type of activity, where, when, how often and with whom you most like to exercise
- · develop a "week at a glance" exercise plan that includes a variety of 3 to 4 activities and has provision for alternate dates and times.

Detail your week plan; highlight today's plan.... what? when? where? with whom?

sun	mon	tue	wed	thur	fri	sat

journal

**Journal below about any temptations, circumstances or emotions – today --
that might keep you from reaching your goals?** (ex: vacation, celebrations, etc)

_____

_____

_____

_____

_____

_____

change
your
life
daily

date _____

e

m

o

t

i

o

n

a

l

forgive

To experience emotional balance on a daily basis, allow one or more of the below questions to prompt you to journal about the relationships in your life that need to heal and be healed.

Today, I know I need to ask _____ to forgive me.

I need to forgive myself for _____

I need to forgive _____ for _____

And I ask God to forgive me for _____

_____

_____

_____

_____

_____

_____

_____

What additional step(s) can I take to complete the healing that I have just journaled about in the above space? (ex: a phone call, letter, apology,etc.)

_____

_____

_____

_____

give

The gift of time, money, resources, or talent to an organization or person is both a powerful and practical way to help others.
What need comes to my mind -- today -- that I can find and fill and/or what person or organization needs a specific source of comfort or encouragement that I can give?

_____

_____

_____

_____

_____

change

your

life

daily

date _____

talk to God

**Today, in honest transparency, share -- in writing – your thoughts,
gratitude, regrets, fears, plans, hopes, dreams and requests
for yourself and others with the living, loving God.**

s
p
i
r
i
t
u
a
l

_____
_____
_____
_____
_____
_____
_____
_____
_____
_____
_____
_____
_____
_____
_____
_____
_____
_____

listen to God

God's voice is found in His word, the Bible.
Unless you have another system, read today's **change your life** **Daily Bible**
using Today's Date. Write in this area, any verse or verses that stand out,
touch your heart, encourage or correct you. **What is God saying to you today?**

_____
_____
_____
_____
_____

change
your
life
daily

date _____

m
e
n
t
a
l

detail your day

appointments

- [ ] quiet time
- [ ] work out
- [ ] _____
- [ ] _____
- [ ] _____
- [ ] _____
- [ ] _____
- [ ] _____
- [ ] _____
- [ ] _____
- [ ] _____
- [ ] _____
- [ ] _____
- [ ] _____
- [ ] _____
- [ ] _____

calls to make   _phone #_

_____
_____
_____
_____
_____

letters to write/fax/email
w f e
- [ ] [ ] [ ] _____
- [ ] [ ] [ ] _____
- [ ] [ ] [ ] _____
- [ ] [ ] [ ] _____

things to do

_____ [ ]
_____ [ ]
_____ [ ]
_____ [ ]
_____ [ ]

define your dream

What is one practical step you can take toward reaching a goal -
and fulfilling a dream - in one or more areas of your life?
Use this space to brainstorm or to develop a dream that won't go away!

physical | emotional
mental | spiritual

change

your

life

daily

date _____

eat right

- · understand your own body type, genetics, metabolism, etc.
- · design a healthy, "plan ahead" eating plan that includes a balance of all the food groups in moderate portions
- · **record your daily intentions for meals and snacks below**
- · **review your progress and make daily adjustments**

breakfast	
lunch	
dinner	
snacks	

exercise regularly

- · determine what type of activity, where, when, how often and with whom you most like to exercise
- · develop a "week at a glance" exercise plan that includes a variety of 3 to 4 activities and has provision for alternate dates and times.

Detail your week plan; highlight today's plan.... what? when? where? with whom?

sun	mon	tue	wed	thur	fri	sat

journal

Journal below about any temptations, circumstances or emotions – today -- that might keep you from reaching your goals? (ex: vacation, celebrations, etc)

_____

_____

_____

_____

_____

_____

p
h
y
s
i
c
a
l

change
your
life
daily

date _____

forgive

To experience emotional balance on a daily basis, allow one or more of the below questions to prompt you to journal about the relationships in your life that need to heal and be healed.

Today, I know I need to ask _____ **to forgive me.**

I need to forgive myself for _____

I need to forgive _____ **for** _____

And I ask God to forgive me for _____

_____

_____

_____

_____

_____

_____

_____

What additional step(s) can I take to complete the healing that I have just journaled about in the above space? (ex: a phone call, letter, apology,etc.)

_____

_____

_____

_____

give

The gift of time, money, resources, or talent to an organization or person is both a powerful and practical way to help others.
What need comes to my mind -- today -- that I can find and fill and/or what person or organization needs a specific source of comfort or encouragement that I can give?

_____

_____

_____

_____

_____

_____

date _____

talk to God

Today, in honest transparency, share -- in writing – your thoughts,
gratitude, regrets, fears, plans, hopes, dreams and requests
for yourself and others with the living, loving God.

_____

_____

_____

_____

_____

_____

_____

_____

_____

_____

_____

_____

_____

_____

_____

_____

_____

s
p
i
r
i
t
u
a
l

listen to God

God's voice is found in His word, the Bible.
Unless you have another system, read today's **change your life Daily Bible**
using Today's Date. Write in this area, any verse or verses that stand out,
touch your heart, encourage or correct you. **What is God saying to you today?**

_____

_____

_____

_____

_____

change
your
life
daily

date _____

m
e
n
t
a
l

detail your day

appointments

☐ *quiet time*
☐ *work out*
☐ _____
☐ _____
☐ _____
☐ _____
☐ _____
☐ _____
☐ _____
☐ _____
☐ _____
☐ _____
☐ _____
☐ _____
☐ _____
☐ _____

calls to make   *phone #*

_____
_____
_____
_____
_____

letters to write/fax/email
w f e

_____ ☐ ☐ ☐
_____ ☐ ☐ ☐
_____ ☐ ☐ ☐
_____ ☐ ☐ ☐

things to do

_____ ☐
_____ ☐
_____ ☐
_____ ☐
_____ ☐

define your dream

What is one practical step you can take toward reaching a goal -
and fulfilling a dream - in one or more areas of your life?
Use this space to brainstorm or to develop a dream that won't go away!

physical	emotional
mental	spiritual

change
your
life
daily

date _____

eat right

- · understand your own body type, genetics, metabolism, etc.
- · design a healthy, "plan ahead" eating plan that includes a balance of all the food groups in moderate portions
- · **record your daily intentions for meals and snacks below**
- · **review your progress and make daily adjustments**

p
h
y
s
i
c
a
l

breakfast _____

_____

lunch _____

_____

dinner _____

_____

snacks _____

exercise regularly

- · determine what type of activity, where, when, how often and with whom you most like to exercise
- · develop a "week at a glance" exercise plan that includes a variety of 3 to 4 activities and has provision for alternate dates and times.

Detail your week plan; highlight today's plan.... what? when? where? with whom?

sun	mon	tue	wed	thur	fri	sat

journal

Journal below about any temptations, circumstances or emotions – today -- that might keep you from reaching your goals? (ex: vacation, celebrations, etc)

_____

_____

_____

_____

_____

_____

change
your
life
daily

date _____

e
m
o
t
i
o
n
a
l

forgive

To experience emotional balance on a daily basis, allow one or more of the below questions to prompt you to journal about the relationships in your life that need to heal and be healed.

Today, I know I need to ask _____ **to forgive me.**

I need to forgive myself for _____

I need to forgive _____ **for** _____

And I ask God to forgive me for _____

_____

_____

_____

_____

_____

_____

_____

What additional step(s) can I take to complete the healing that I have just journaled about in the above space? (ex: a phone call, letter, apology,etc.)

_____

_____

_____

give

The gift of time, money, resources, or talent to an organization or person is both a powerful and practical way to help others.
What need comes to my mind -- today -- that I can find and fill and/or what person or organization needs a specific source of comfort or encouragement that I can give?

_____

_____

_____

_____

_____

change

your

life

daily

date _____

talk to God

Today, in honest transparency, share -- in writing – your thoughts,
gratitude, regrets, fears, plans, hopes, dreams and requests
for yourself and others with the living, loving God.

s
p
i
r
i
t
u
a
l

_____
_____
_____
_____
_____
_____
_____
_____
_____
_____
_____
_____
_____
_____
_____
_____
_____
_____
_____

listen to God

God's voice is found in His word, the Bible.
Unless you have another system, read today's **change your life** **Daily Bible**
using Today's Date. Write in this area, any verse or verses that stand out,
touch your heart, encourage or correct you. **What is God saying to you today?**

_____
_____
_____
_____
_____
_____

change
your
life
daily

date _____

m
e
n
t
a
l

detail your day

appointments

quiet time	☐
work out	☐
	☐
	☐
	☐
	☐
	☐
	☐
	☐
	☐
	☐
	☐
	☐
	☐
	☐
	☐

calls to make   *phone #*

_____
_____
_____
_____
_____

letters to write/fax/email
w   f   e

☐ ☐ ☐
☐ ☐ ☐
☐ ☐ ☐
☐ ☐ ☐

things to do

	☐
	☐
	☐
	☐
	☐

define your dream

What is one practical step you can take toward reaching a goal -
and fulfilling a dream - in one or more areas of your life?
Use this space to brainstorm or to develop a dream that won't go away!

physical	emotional
mental	spiritual

change
your
life
daily

date _____

eat right

- understand your own body type, genetics, metabolism, etc.
- design a healthy, "plan ahead" eating plan that includes a balance of all the food groups in moderate portions
- **record your daily intentions for meals and snacks below**
- **review your progress and make daily adjustments**

breakfast	
lunch	
dinner	
snacks	

exercise regularly

- determine what type of activity, where, when, how often and with whom you most like to exercise
- develop a "week at a glance" exercise plan that includes a variety of 3 to 4 activities and has provision for alternate dates and times.

Detail your week plan; highlight today's plan.... what? when? where? with whom?

sun	mon	tue	wed	thur	fri	sat

journal

Journal below about any temptations, circumstances or emotions – today -- that might keep you from reaching your goals? (ex: vacation, celebrations, etc)

_____

_____

_____

_____

_____

_____

p h y s i c a l

change your life daily

date _____

e
m
o
t
i
o
n
a
l

forgive

To experience emotional balance on a daily basis, allow one or more of the below questions to prompt you to journal about the relationships in your life that need to heal and be healed.

Today, I know I need to ask _____ **to forgive me.**

I need to forgive myself for _____

I need to forgive _____ **for** _____

And I ask God to forgive me for _____

_____

_____

_____

_____

_____

_____

What additional step(s) can I take to complete the healing that I have just journaled about in the above space? (ex: a phone call, letter, apology, etc.)

_____

_____

_____

give

The gift of time, money, resources, or talent to an organization or person is both a powerful and practical way to help others.
What need comes to my mind -- today -- that I can find and fill and/or what person or organization needs a specific source of comfort or encouragement that I can give?

_____

_____

_____

_____

_____

change
your
life
daily

date _____

talk to God

Today, in honest transparency, share -- in writing – your thoughts, gratitude, regrets, fears, plans, hopes, dreams and requests for yourself and others with the living, loving God.

s
p
i
r
i
t
u
a
l

_____

_____

_____

_____

_____

_____

_____

_____

_____

_____

_____

_____

_____

_____

_____

_____

_____

_____

listen to God

God's voice is found in His word, the Bible.
Unless you have another system, read today's **change your life Daily Bible**
using Today's Date. Write in this area, any verse or verses that stand out,
touch your heart, encourage or correct you. **What is God saying to you today?**

_____

_____

_____

_____

_____

_____

change
your
life
daily

date _____

m
e
n
t
a
l

detail your day

appointments

quiet time	☐
work out	☐
	☐
	☐
	☐
	☐
	☐
	☐
	☐
	☐
	☐
	☐
	☐
	☐
	☐
	☐
	☐

calls to make   *phone #*

_____

_____

_____

_____

_____

letters to write/fax/email
                                        w   f   e
_____ ☐ ☐ ☐

_____ ☐ ☐ ☐

_____ ☐ ☐ ☐

_____ ☐ ☐ ☐

things to do

_____ ☐

_____ ☐

_____ ☐

_____ ☐

_____ ☐

define your dream

What is one practical step you can take toward reaching a goal -
and fulfilling a dream - in one or more areas of your life?
Use this space to brainstorm or to develop a dream that won't go away!

physical | emotional

mental | spiritual

change

your

life

daily

date _____

eat right

- · understand your own body type, genetics, metabolism, etc.
- · design a healthy, "plan ahead" eating plan that includes a balance of all the food groups in moderate portions
- · **record your daily intentions for meals and snacks below**
- · **review your progress and make daily adjustments**

p
h
y
s
i
c
a
l

breakfast	
lunch	
dinner	
snacks	

exercise regularly

- · determine what type of activity, where, when, how often and with whom you most like to exercise
- · develop a "week at a glance" exercise plan that includes a variety of 3 to 4 activities and has provision for alternate dates and times.

Detail your week plan; highlight today's plan.... what? when? where? with whom?

| sun | mon | tue | wed | thur | fri | sat |

journal

Journal below about any temptations, circumstances or emotions – today -- that might keep you from reaching your goals? (ex: vacation, celebrations, etc)

change
your
life
daily

date _____

e
m
o
t
i
o
n
a
l

forgive

To experience emotional balance on a daily basis, allow one or more of the below questions to prompt you to journal about the relationships in your life that need to heal and be healed.

Today, I know I need to ask _____ **to forgive me.**

I need to forgive myself for _____

I need to forgive _____ **for** _____

And I ask God to forgive me for _____

_____

_____

_____

_____

_____

_____

What additional step(s) can I take to complete the healing that I have just journaled about in the above space? (ex: a phone call, letter, apology,etc.)

_____

_____

_____

_____

give

The gift of time, money, resources, or talent to an organization or person is both a powerful and practical way to help others.
What need comes to my mind -- today -- that I can find and fill and/or what person or organization needs a specific source of comfort or encouragement that I can give?

_____

_____

_____

_____

_____

_____

change
your
life
daily

date _____

talk to God

Today, in honest transparency, share -- in writing – your thoughts, gratitude, regrets, fears, plans, hopes, dreams and requests for yourself and others with the living, loving God.

s
p
i
r
i
t
u
a
l

_____
_____
_____
_____
_____
_____
_____
_____
_____
_____
_____
_____
_____
_____
_____
_____
_____
_____
_____

listen to God

God's voice is found in His word, the Bible.
Unless you have another system, read today's **change your life Daily Bible** using Today's Date. Write in this area, any verse or verses that stand out, touch your heart, encourage or correct you. **What is God saying to you today?**

_____
_____
_____
_____
_____
_____

change
your
life
daily

date _____

m
e
n
t
a
l

detail your day

appointments

quiet time	☐
work out	☐
	☐
	☐
	☐
	☐
	☐
	☐
	☐
	☐
	☐
	☐
	☐
	☐
	☐
	☐
	☐

calls to make   *phone #*

_____
_____
_____
_____
_____

letters to write/fax/email
w   f   e
☐ ☐ ☐
☐ ☐ ☐
☐ ☐ ☐
☐ ☐ ☐

things to do

_____	☐
_____	☐
_____	☐
_____	☐
_____	☐

define your dream

What is one practical step you can take toward reaching a goal -
and fulfilling a dream - in one or more areas of your life?
Use this space to brainstorm or to develop a dream that won't go away!

physical | emotional

mental | spiritual

change
your
life
daily

date _____

eat right

- understand your own body type, genetics, metabolism, etc.
- design a healthy, "plan ahead" eating plan that includes a balance of all the food groups in moderate portions
- **record your daily intentions for meals and snacks below**
- **review your progress and make daily adjustments**

breakfast
_____

lunch
_____

dinner
_____

snacks
_____

exercise regularly

- determine what type of activity, where, when, how often and with whom you most like to exercise
- develop a "week at a glance" exercise plan that includes a variety of 3 to 4 activities and has provision for alternate dates and times.

Detail your week plan; highlight today's plan.... what? when? where? with whom?

sun	mon	tue	wed	thur	fri	sat

journal

Journal below about any temptations, circumstances or emotions – today -- that might keep you from reaching your goals? (ex: vacation, celebrations, etc)

_____

_____

_____

_____

_____

p
h
y
s
i
c
a
l

change
your
life
daily

date _____

e
m
o
t
i
o
n
a
l

forgive

To experience emotional balance on a daily basis, allow one or more of the below questions to prompt you to journal about the relationships in your life that need to heal and be healed.

Today, I know I need to ask _____ **to forgive me.**

I need to forgive myself for _____

I need to forgive _____ **for** _____

And I ask God to forgive me for _____

_____

_____

_____

_____

_____

_____

What additional step(s) can I take to complete the healing that I have just journaled about in the above space? (ex: a phone call, letter, apology,etc.)

_____

_____

_____

give

The gift of time, money, resources, or talent to an organization or person is both a powerful and practical way to help others.
What need comes to my mind -- today -- that I can find and fill and/or what person or organization needs a specific source of comfort or encouragement that I can give?

_____

_____

_____

_____

_____

change
your
life
daily

date _____

talk to God

Today, in honest transparency, share -- in writing – your thoughts, gratitude, regrets, fears, plans, hopes, dreams and requests for yourself and others with the living, loving God.

s
p
i
r
i
t
u
a
l

_____
_____
_____
_____
_____
_____
_____
_____
_____
_____
_____
_____
_____
_____
_____
_____
_____
_____
_____

listen to God

God's voice is found in His word, the Bible.
Unless you have another system, read today's **change your life Daily Bible** using Today's Date. Write in this area, any verse or verses that stand out, touch your heart, encourage or correct you. **What is God saying to you today?**

_____
_____
_____
_____
_____
_____

change
your
life
daily

date _____

m
e
n
t
a
l

detail your day

appointments

quiet time ☐
work out ☐
_____ ☐
_____ ☐
_____ ☐
_____ ☐
_____ ☐
_____ ☐
_____ ☐
_____ ☐
_____ ☐
_____ ☐
_____ ☐
_____ ☐
_____ ☐
_____ ☐
_____ ☐

calls to make   *phone #*

_____
_____
_____
_____
_____
_____

letters to write/fax/email
                     w   f   e
                    ☐ ☐ ☐
_____ ☐ ☐ ☐
_____ ☐ ☐ ☐
_____ ☐ ☐ ☐
_____ ☐ ☐ ☐

things to do

_____ ☐
_____ ☐
_____ ☐
_____ ☐
_____ ☐
_____ ☐

define your dream

What is one practical step you can take toward reaching a goal -
and fulfilling a dream - in one or more areas of your life?
Use this space to brainstorm or to develop a dream that won't go away!

physical | emotional
mental | spiritual

change
your
life
daily

date _____

eat right

- · understand your own body type, genetics, metabolism, etc.
- · design a healthy, "plan ahead" eating plan that includes a balance of all the food groups in moderate portions
- · **record your daily intentions for meals and snacks below**
- · **review your progress and make daily adjustments**

breakfast	
lunch	
dinner	
snacks	

exercise regularly

- · determine what type of activity, where, when, how often and with whom you most like to exercise
- · develop a "week at a glance" exercise plan that includes a variety of 3 to 4 activities and has provision for alternate dates and times.

Detail your week plan; highlight today's plan . . . what? when? where? with whom?

sun	mon	tue	wed	thur	fri	sat

journal

Journal below about any temptations, circumstances or emotions – today -- that might keep you from reaching your goals? (ex: vacation, celebrations, etc)

_____

_____

_____

_____

_____

_____

p
h
y
s
i
c
a
l

change
your
life
daily

date _____

e
m
o
t
i
o
n
a
l

forgive

To experience emotional balance on a daily basis, allow one or more of the below questions to prompt you to journal about the relationships in your life that need to heal and be healed.

Today, I know I need to ask _____ **to forgive me.**

I need to forgive myself for _____

I need to forgive _____ **for** _____

And I ask God to forgive me for _____

_____

_____

_____

_____

_____

_____

What additional step(s) can I take to complete the healing that I have just journaled about in the above space? (ex: a phone call, letter, apology,etc.)

_____

_____

_____

_____

give

The gift of time, money, resources, or talent to an organization or person is both a powerful and practical way to help others.
What need comes to my mind -- today -- that I can find and fill and/or what person or organization needs a specific source of comfort or encouragement that I can give?

_____

_____

_____

_____

_____

change
your
life
daily

date _____

talk to God

**Today, in honest transparency, share -- in writing – your thoughts,
gratitude, regrets, fears, plans, hopes, dreams and requests
for yourself and others with the living, loving God.**

s
p
i
r
i
t
u
a
l

_____
_____
_____
_____
_____
_____
_____
_____
_____
_____
_____
_____
_____
_____
_____
_____
_____
_____

listen to God

God's voice is found in His word, the Bible.
Unless you have another system, read today's **change your life** **Daily Bible**
using Today's Date. Write in this area, any verse or verses that stand out,
touch your heart, encourage or correct you. **What is God saying to you today?**

_____
_____
_____
_____
_____

change
your
life
daily

date _____

m
e
n
t
a
l

detail your day

appointments

- quiet time ☐
- work out ☐
- _____ ☐
- _____ ☐
- _____ ☐
- _____ ☐
- _____ ☐
- _____ ☐
- _____ ☐
- _____ ☐
- _____ ☐
- _____ ☐
- _____ ☐
- _____ ☐
- _____ ☐
- _____ ☐
- _____ ☐
- _____ ☐

calls to make   *phone #*

- _____
- _____
- _____
- _____
- _____

letters to write/fax/email
w   f   e
- _____ ☐ ☐ ☐
- _____ ☐ ☐ ☐
- _____ ☐ ☐ ☐
- _____ ☐ ☐ ☐

things to do

- _____ ☐
- _____ ☐
- _____ ☐
- _____ ☐
- _____ ☐

define your dream

What is one practical step you can take toward reaching a goal -
and fulfilling a dream - in one or more areas of your life?
Use this space to brainstorm or to develop a dream that won't go away!

physical | emotional
mental | spiritual

change
your
life
daily

date _____

eat right

- understand your own body type, genetics, metabolism, etc.
- design a healthy, "plan ahead" eating plan that includes a balance of all the food groups in moderate portions
- **record your daily intentions for meals and snacks below**
- **review your progress and make daily adjustments**

breakfast _____

lunch _____

dinner _____

snacks _____

p
h
y
s
i
c
a
l

exercise regularly

- determine what type of activity, where, when, how often and with whom you most like to exercise
- develop a "week at a glance" exercise plan that includes a variety of 3 to 4 activities and has provision for alternate dates and times.

Detail your week plan; highlight today's plan.... what? when? where? with whom?

sun	mon	tue	wed	thur	fri	sat

journal

Journal below about any temptations, circumstances or emotions – today -- that might keep you from reaching your goals? (ex: vacation, celebrations, etc)

_____

_____

_____

_____

_____

change
your
life
daily

date _____

e m o t i o n a l

forgive

To experience emotional balance on a daily basis, allow one or more of the below questions to prompt you to journal about the relationships in your life that need to heal and be healed.

Today, I know I need to ask _____ **to forgive me.**

I need to forgive myself for _____

I need to forgive _____ **for** _____

And I ask God to forgive me for _____

_____
_____
_____
_____
_____
_____

What additional step(s) can I take to complete the healing that I have just journaled about in the above space? (ex: a phone call, letter, apology,etc.)

_____
_____
_____
_____

give

The gift of time, money, resources, or talent to an organization or person is both a powerful and practical way to help others.
What need comes to my mind -- today -- that I can find and fill and/or what person or organization needs a specific source of comfort or encouragement that I can give?

_____
_____
_____
_____
_____
_____

change
your
life
daily

date _____

talk to God

Today, in honest transparency, share -- in writing – your thoughts, gratitude, regrets, fears, plans, hopes, dreams and requests for yourself and others with the living, loving God.

s
p
i
r
i
t
u
a
l

_____
_____
_____
_____
_____
_____
_____
_____
_____
_____
_____
_____
_____
_____
_____
_____
_____
_____
_____
_____

listen to God

God's voice is found in His word, the Bible.
Unless you have another system, read today's **change your life Daily Bible** using Today's Date. Write in this area, any verse or verses that stand out, touch your heart, encourage or correct you. **What is God saying to you today?**

_____
_____
_____
_____
_____
_____

change
your
life
daily

date _____

m e n t a l

detail your day

appointments

quiet time	☐
work out	☐
	☐
	☐
	☐
	☐
	☐
	☐
	☐
	☐
	☐
	☐
	☐
	☐
	☐
	☐

calls to make   *phone #*

_____

_____

_____

_____

_____

letters to write/fax/email
w   f   e

_____ ☐ ☐ ☐

_____ ☐ ☐ ☐

_____ ☐ ☐ ☐

_____ ☐ ☐ ☐

things to do

_____ ☐

_____ ☐

_____ ☐

_____ ☐

_____ ☐

define your dream

What is one practical step you can take toward reaching a goal -
and fulfilling a dream - in one or more areas of your life?
Use this space to brainstorm or to develop a dream that won't go away!

physical	emotional
mental	spiritual

change

your

life

daily

date _____

eat right

- · understand your own body type, genetics, metabolism, etc.
- · design a healthy, "plan ahead" eating plan that includes a balance of all the food groups in moderate portions
- · **record your daily intentions for meals and snacks below**
- · **review your progress and make daily adjustments**

breakfast	
lunch	
dinner	
snacks	

exercise regularly

- · determine what type of activity, where, when, how often and with whom you most like to exercise
- · develop a "week at a glance" exercise plan that includes a variety of 3 to 4 activities and has provision for alternate dates and times.

Detail your week plan; highlight today's plan.... what? when? where? with whom?

sun	mon	tue	wed	thur	fri	sat

journal

Journal below about any temptations, circumstances or emotions – today -- that might keep you from reaching your goals? (ex: vacation, celebrations, etc)

_____

_____

_____

_____

_____

p
h
y
s
i
c
a
l

change
your
life
daily

date _____

forgive

To experience emotional balance on a daily basis, allow one or more of the below questions to prompt you to journal about the relationships in your life that need to heal and be healed.

Today, I know I need to ask _____ **to forgive me.**

I need to forgive myself for _____

I need to forgive _____ **for** _____

And I ask God to forgive me for _____

_____

_____

_____

_____

_____

_____

What additional step(s) can I take to complete the healing that I have just journaled about in the above space? (ex: a phone call, letter, apology,etc.)

_____

_____

_____

_____

give

The gift of time, money, resources, or talent to an organization or person is both a powerful and practical way to help others.
What need comes to my mind -- today -- that I can find and fill and/or what person or organization needs a specific source of comfort or encouragement that I can give?

_____

_____

_____

_____

_____

_____

date _____

talk to God

Today, in honest transparency, share -- in writing – your thoughts, gratitude, regrets, fears, plans, hopes, dreams and requests for yourself and others with the living, loving God.

_____

_____

_____

_____

_____

_____

_____

_____

_____

_____

_____

_____

_____

_____

_____

_____

_____

_____

s
p
i
r
i
t
u
a
l

listen to God

God's voice is found in His word, the Bible.
Unless you have another system, read today's **change your life Daily Bible** using Today's Date. Write in this area, any verse or verses that stand out, touch your heart, encourage or correct you. **What is God saying to you today?**

_____

_____

_____

_____

_____

_____

change
your
life
daily

date _____

m
e
n
t
a
l

detail your day

appointments

quiet time	☐
work out	☐
	☐
	☐
	☐
	☐
	☐
	☐
	☐
	☐
	☐
	☐
	☐
	☐
	☐
	☐

calls to make   *phone #*

_____

_____

_____

_____

letters to write/fax/email
w   f   e

_____ ☐ ☐ ☐

_____ ☐ ☐ ☐

_____ ☐ ☐ ☐

_____ ☐ ☐ ☐

things to do

_____ ☐

_____ ☐

_____ ☐

_____ ☐

_____ ☐

define your dream

What is one practical step you can take toward reaching a goal -
and fulfilling a dream - in one or more areas of your life?
Use this space to brainstorm or to develop a dream that won't go away!

physical	emotional
mental	spiritual

change
your
life
daily

date _____

eat right

- · understand your own body type, genetics, metabolism, etc.
- · design a healthy, "plan ahead" eating plan that includes a balance of all the food groups in moderate portions
- · **record your daily intentions for meals and snacks below**
- · **review your progress and make daily adjustments**

breakfast	
lunch	
dinner	
snacks	

exercise regularly

- · determine what type of activity, where, when, how often and with whom you most like to exercise
- · develop a "week at a glance" exercise plan that includes a variety of 3 to 4 activities and has provision for alternate dates and times.

Detail your week plan; highlight today's plan.... what? when? where? with whom?

sun	mon	tue	wed	thur	fri	sat

journal

Journal below about any temptations, circumstances or emotions – today -- that might keep you from reaching your goals? (ex: vacation, celebrations, etc)

_____

_____

_____

_____

_____

_____

p
h
y
s
i
c
a
l

change
your
life
daily

date _____

e
m
o
t
i
o
n
a
l

forgive

To experience emotional balance on a daily basis, allow one or more of the below questions to prompt you to journal about the relationships in your life that need to heal and be healed.

Today, I know I need to ask _____ **to forgive me.**

I need to forgive myself for _____

I need to forgive _____ **for** _____

And I ask God to forgive me for _____

_____

_____

_____

_____

_____

_____

What additional step(s) can I take to complete the healing that I have just journaled about in the above space? (ex: a phone call, letter, apology,etc.)

_____

_____

_____

_____

give

The gift of time, money, resources, or talent to an organization or person is both a powerful and practical way to help others.
What need comes to my mind -- today -- that I can find and fill and/or what person or organization needs a specific source of comfort or encouragement that I can give?

_____

_____

_____

_____

_____

change
your
life
daily

date _____

talk to God

Today, in honest transparency, share -- in writing – your thoughts,
gratitude, regrets, fears, plans, hopes, dreams and requests
for yourself and others with the living, loving God.

s
p
i
r
i
t
u
a
l

_____

_____

_____

_____

_____

_____

_____

_____

_____

_____

_____

_____

_____

_____

_____

_____

_____

_____

listen to God

God's voice is found in His word, the Bible.
Unless you have another system, read today's **change your life** **Daily Bible**
using Today's Date. Write in this area, any verse or verses that stand out,
touch your heart, encourage or correct you. **What is God saying to you today?**

_____

_____

_____

_____

_____

_____

change
your
life
daily

date _____

m
e
n
t
a
l

detail your day

appointments

- quiet time ☐
- work out ☐
- _____ ☐
- _____ ☐
- _____ ☐
- _____ ☐
- _____ ☐
- _____ ☐
- _____ ☐
- _____ ☐
- _____ ☐
- _____ ☐
- _____ ☐
- _____ ☐
- _____ ☐
- _____ ☐
- _____ ☐
- _____ ☐

calls to make   *phone #*

- _____
- _____
- _____
- _____

letters to write/fax/email
w   f   e

- _____ ☐ ☐ ☐
- _____ ☐ ☐ ☐
- _____ ☐ ☐ ☐
- _____ ☐ ☐ ☐

things to do

- _____ ☐
- _____ ☐
- _____ ☐
- _____ ☐
- _____ ☐

define your dream

What is one practical step you can take toward reaching a goal -
and fulfilling a dream - in one or more areas of your life?
Use this space to brainstorm or to develop a dream that won't go away!

physical | emotional
mental | spiritual

change
your
life
daily

date _____

eat right

- · understand your own body type, genetics, metabolism, etc.
- · design a healthy, "plan ahead" eating plan that includes a balance of all the food groups in moderate portions
- · **record your daily intentions for meals and snacks below**
- · **review your progress and make daily adjustments**

breakfast	
lunch	
dinner	
snacks	

exercise regularly

- · determine what type of activity, where, when, how often and with whom you most like to exercise
- · develop a "week at a glance" exercise plan that includes a variety of 3 to 4 activities and has provision for alternate dates and times.

Detail your week plan; highlight today's plan   what? when? where? with whom?

sun	mon	tue	wed	thur	fri	sat

journal

Journal below about any temptations, circumstances or emotions – today -- that might keep you from reaching your goals? (ex: vacation, celebrations, etc)

_____

_____

_____

_____

_____

_____

p
h
y
s
i
c
a
l

change
your
life
daily

date _____

e
m
o
t
i
o
n
a
l

forgive

To experience emotional balance on a daily basis, allow one or more of the below questions to prompt you to journal about the relationships in your life that need to heal and be healed.

Today, I know I need to ask _____ **to forgive me.**

I need to forgive myself for _____

I need to forgive _____ **for** _____

And I ask God to forgive me for _____

_____

_____

_____

_____

_____

_____

What additional step(s) can I take to complete the healing that I have just journaled about in the above space? (ex: a phone call, letter, apology,etc.)

_____

_____

_____

give

The gift of time, money, resources, or talent to an organization or person is both a powerful and practical way to help others.
What need comes to my mind -- today -- that I can find and fill and/or what person or organization needs a specific source of comfort or encouragement that I can give?

_____

_____

_____

_____

_____

change
your
life
daily

date _____

talk to God

Today, in honest transparency, share -- in writing – your thoughts, gratitude, regrets, fears, plans, hopes, dreams and requests for yourself and others with the living, loving God.

s
p
i
r
i
t
u
a
l

listen to God

God's voice is found in His word, the Bible.
Unless you have another system, read today's **change your life** **Daily Bible** using Today's Date. Write in this area, any verse or verses that stand out, touch your heart, encourage or correct you. **What is God saying to you today?**

change
your
life
daily

date _____

m
e
n
t
a
l

detail your day

appointments

quiet time ☐
work out ☐
_____ ☐
_____ ☐
_____ ☐
_____ ☐
_____ ☐
_____ ☐
_____ ☐
_____ ☐
_____ ☐
_____ ☐
_____ ☐
_____ ☐
_____ ☐
_____ ☐

calls to make   *phone #*

_____
_____
_____
_____
_____

letters to write/fax/email
w   f   e
☐ ☐ ☐
☐ ☐ ☐
☐ ☐ ☐
☐ ☐ ☐

things to do

_____ ☐
_____ ☐
_____ ☐
_____ ☐
_____ ☐

define your dream

What is one practical step you can take toward reaching a goal -
and fulfilling a dream - in one or more areas of your life?
Use this space to brainstorm or to develop a dream that won't go away!

physical | emotional
mental | spiritual

change
your
life
daily

date _____

eat right

- · understand your own body type, genetics, metabolism, etc.
- · design a healthy, "plan ahead" eating plan that includes a balance of all the food groups in moderate portions
- · **record your daily intentions for meals and snacks below**
- · **review your progress and make daily adjustments**

breakfast	
lunch	
dinner	
snacks	

exercise regularly

- · determine what type of activity, where, when, how often and with whom you most like to exercise
- · develop a "week at a glance" exercise plan that includes a variety of 3 to 4 activities and has provision for alternate dates and times.

Detail your week plan; highlight today's plan.... what? when? where? with whom?

sun	mon	tue	wed	thur	fri	sat

journal

Journal below about any temptations, circumstances or emotions – today -- that might keep you from reaching your goals? (ex: vacation, celebrations, etc)

_____

_____

_____

_____

_____

_____

p h y s i c a l

change
your
life
daily

date _____

e
m
o
t
i
o
n
a
l

forgive

To experience emotional balance on a daily basis, allow one or more of the below questions to prompt you to journal about the relationships in your life that need to heal and be healed.

Today, I know I need to ask _____ **to forgive me.**

I need to forgive myself for _____

I need to forgive _____ **for** _____

And I ask God to forgive me for _____

_____

_____

_____

_____

_____

_____

_____

What additional step(s) can I take to complete the healing that I have just journaled about in the above space? (ex: a phone call, letter, apology,etc.)

_____

_____

_____

_____

give

The gift of time, money, resources, or talent to an organization or person is both a powerful and practical way to help others.
What need comes to my mind -- today -- that I can find and fill and/or what person or organization needs a specific source of comfort or encouragement that I can give?

_____

_____

_____

_____

_____

_____

change
your
life
daily

date _____

talk to God

Today, in honest transparency, share -- in writing – your thoughts, gratitude, regrets, fears, plans, hopes, dreams and requests for yourself and others with the living, loving God.

_____
_____
_____
_____
_____
_____
_____
_____
_____
_____
_____
_____
_____
_____
_____
_____
_____
_____
_____

s
p
i
r
i
t
u
a
l

listen to God

God's voice is found in His word, the Bible.
Unless you have another system, read today's **change your life Daily Bible** using Today's Date. Write in this area, any verse or verses that stand out, touch your heart, encourage or correct you. **What is God saying to you today?**

_____
_____
_____
_____
_____
_____
_____

change
your
life
daily

date _____

m
e
n
t
a
l

detail your day

appointments

quiet time ☐
work out ☐
_____ ☐
_____ ☐
_____ ☐
_____ ☐
_____ ☐
_____ ☐
_____ ☐
_____ ☐
_____ ☐
_____ ☐
_____ ☐
_____ ☐
_____ ☐
_____ ☐
_____ ☐

calls to make   *phone #*

_____
_____
_____
_____
_____

letters to write/fax/email
w   f   e
_____ ☐ ☐ ☐
_____ ☐ ☐ ☐
_____ ☐ ☐ ☐
_____ ☐ ☐ ☐

things to do

_____ ☐
_____ ☐
_____ ☐
_____ ☐
_____ ☐

define your dream

What is one practical step you can take toward reaching a goal -
and fulfilling a dream - in one or more areas of your life?
Use this space to brainstorm or to develop a dream that won't go away!

physical | emotional
mental | spiritual

change
your
life
daily

date _____

eat right

· understand your own body type, genetics, metabolism, etc.
· design a healthy, "plan ahead" eating plan that includes a balance
   of all the food groups in moderate portions
· **record your daily intentions for meals and snacks below**
· **review your progress and make daily adjustments**

breakfast	
lunch	
dinner	
snacks	

exercise regularly

· determine what type of activity, where, when, how often and with whom you
   most like to exercise
· develop a "week at a glance" exercise plan that includes a variety of 3 to 4 activities
   and has provision for alternate dates and times.

Detail your week plan; highlight today's plan.... what? when? where? with whom?

sun	mon	tue	wed	thur	fri	sat

journal

**Journal below about any temptations, circumstances or emotions – today --
that might keep you from reaching your goals?** (ex: vacation, celebrations, etc)

_____
_____
_____
_____
_____
_____

p
h
y
s
i
c
a
l

change
your
life
daily

date _____

e
m
o
t
i
o
n
a
l

forgive

To experience emotional balance on a daily basis, allow one or more of the below questions to prompt you to journal about the relationships in your life that need to heal and be healed.

Today, I know I need to ask _____ **to forgive me.**

I need to forgive myself for _____

I need to forgive _____ **for** _____

And I ask God to forgive me for _____

_____

_____

_____

_____

_____

_____

What additional step(s) can I take to complete the healing that I have just journaled about in the above space? (ex: a phone call, letter, apology, etc.)

_____

_____

_____

_____

give

The gift of time, money, resources, or talent to an organization or person is both a powerful and practical way to help others.
What need comes to my mind -- today -- that I can find and fill and/or what person or organization needs a specific source of comfort or encouragement that I can give?

_____

_____

_____

_____

_____

_____

change
your
life
daily

date _____

talk to God

Today, in honest transparency, share -- in writing – your thoughts, gratitude, regrets, fears, plans, hopes, dreams and requests for yourself and others with the living, loving God.

s
p
i
r
i
t
u
a
l

_____

_____

_____

_____

_____

_____

_____

_____

_____

_____

_____

_____

_____

_____

_____

_____

_____

_____

listen to God

God's voice is found in His word, the Bible.
Unless you have another system, read today's **change your life Daily Bible**
using Today's Date. Write in this area, any verse or verses that stand out,
touch your heart, encourage or correct you. **What is God saying to you today?**

_____

_____

_____

_____

_____

_____

change
your
life
daily

date _____

m
e
n
t
a
l

detail your day

appointments

quiet time ☐

work out ☐

_____ ☐

_____ ☐

_____ ☐

_____ ☐

_____ ☐

_____ ☐

_____ ☐

_____ ☐

_____ ☐

_____ ☐

_____ ☐

_____ ☐

_____ ☐

_____ ☐

calls to make   *phone #*

_____

_____

_____

_____

_____

letters to write/fax/email
                              w   f   e

_____   ☐ ☐ ☐

_____   ☐ ☐ ☐

_____   ☐ ☐ ☐

_____   ☐ ☐ ☐

things to do

_____ ☐

_____ ☐

_____ ☐

_____ ☐

_____ ☐

define your dream

What is one practical step you can take toward reaching a goal -
and fulfilling a dream - in one or more areas of your life?
Use this space to brainstorm or to develop a dream that won't go away!

physical | emotional

mental | spiritual

change
your
life
daily

date _____

eat right

- understand your own body type, genetics, metabolism, etc.
- design a healthy, "plan ahead" eating plan that includes a balance of all the food groups in moderate portions
- **record your daily intentions for meals and snacks below**
- **review your progress and make daily adjustments**

p
h
y
s
i
c
a
l

breakfast _____

lunch _____

dinner _____

snacks _____

exercise regularly

- determine what type of activity, where, when, how often and with whom you most like to exercise
- develop a "week at a glance" exercise plan that includes a variety of 3 to 4 activities and has provision for alternate dates and times.

Detail your week plan; highlight today's plan.... what? when? where? with whom?

sun	mon	tue	wed	thur	fri	sat

journal

Journal below about any temptations, circumstances or emotions – today -- that might keep you from reaching your goals? (ex: vacation, celebrations, etc)

_____

_____

_____

_____

_____

_____

change
your
life
daily

date _____

e
m
o
t
i
o
n
a
l

forgive

To experience emotional balance on a daily basis, allow one or more of the below questions to prompt you to journal about the relationships in your life that need to heal and be healed.

Today, I know I need to ask _____ to forgive me.

I need to forgive myself for _____

I need to forgive _____ for _____

And I ask God to forgive me for _____

_____

_____

_____

_____

_____

_____

_____

What additional step(s) can I take to complete the healing that I have just journaled about in the above space? (ex: a phone call, letter, apology,etc.)

_____

_____

_____

_____

give

The gift of time, money, resources, or talent to an organization or person is both a powerful and practical way to help others.
What need comes to my mind -- today -- that I can find and fill and/or what person or organization needs a specific source of comfort or encouragement that I can give?

_____

_____

_____

_____

_____

_____

change
your
life
daily

date _____

talk to God

Today, in honest transparency, share -- in writing – your thoughts, gratitude, regrets, fears, plans, hopes, dreams and requests for yourself and others with the living, loving God.

_____
_____
_____
_____
_____
_____
_____
_____
_____
_____
_____
_____
_____
_____
_____
_____
_____
_____
_____
_____
_____

s
p
i
r
i
t
u
a
l

listen to God

God's voice is found in His word, the Bible.
Unless you have another system, read today's **change your life Daily Bible**
using Today's Date. Write in this area, any verse or verses that stand out,
touch your heart, encourage or correct you. **What is God saying to you today?**

_____
_____
_____
_____
_____
_____

change
your
life
daily

date _____

m
e
n
t
a
l

detail your day

appointments

quiet time ☐
work out ☐
_____ ☐
_____ ☐
_____ ☐
_____ ☐
_____ ☐
_____ ☐
_____ ☐
_____ ☐
_____ ☐
_____ ☐
_____ ☐
_____ ☐
_____ ☐
_____ ☐

calls to make   *phone #*

_____
_____
_____
_____
_____

letters to write/fax/email
w f e
☐ ☐ ☐
☐ ☐ ☐
☐ ☐ ☐
☐ ☐ ☐

things to do

_____ ☐
_____ ☐
_____ ☐
_____ ☐
_____ ☐

define your dream

What is one practical step you can take toward reaching a goal -
and fulfilling a dream - in one or more areas of your life?
Use this space to brainstorm or to develop a dream that won't go away!

physical | emotional
mental | spiritual

change
your
life
daily

date _____

eat right

- · understand your own body type, genetics, metabolism, etc.
- · design a healthy, "plan ahead" eating plan that includes a balance of all the food groups in moderate portions
- · **record your daily intentions for meals and snacks below**
- · **review your progress and make daily adjustments**

breakfast	
lunch	
dinner	
snacks	

exercise regularly

- · determine what type of activity, where, when, how often and with whom you most like to exercise
- · develop a "week at a glance" exercise plan that includes a variety of 3 to 4 activities and has provision for alternate dates and times.

Detail your week plan; highlight today's plan.... what? when? where? with whom?

sun	mon	tue	wed	thur	fri	sat

journal

Journal below about any temptations, circumstances or emotions – today -- that might keep you from reaching your goals? (ex: vacation, celebrations, etc)

_____
_____
_____
_____
_____
_____

p
h
y
s
i
c
a
l

change
your
life
daily

date _____

e
m
o
t
i
o
n
a
l

forgive

To experience emotional balance on a daily basis, allow one or more of the below questions to prompt you to journal about the relationships in your life that need to heal and be healed.

Today, I know I need to ask _____ **to forgive me.**

I need to forgive myself for _____

I need to forgive _____ **for** _____

And I ask God to forgive me for _____

_____

_____

_____

_____

_____

_____

_____

What additional step(s) can I take to complete the healing that I have just journaled about in the above space? (ex: a phone call, letter, apology,etc.)

_____

_____

_____

give

The gift of time, money, resources, or talent to an organization or person is both a powerful and practical way to help others.
What need comes to my mind -- today -- that I can find and fill and/or what person or organization needs a specific source of comfort or encouragement that I can give?

_____

_____

_____

_____

change
your
life
daily

date _____

talk to God

Today, in honest transparency, share -- in writing – your thoughts,
gratitude, regrets, fears, plans, hopes, dreams and requests
for yourself and others with the living, loving God.

_____

_____

_____

_____

_____

_____

_____

_____

_____

_____

_____

_____

_____

_____

_____

_____

_____

_____

s
p
i
r
i
t
u
a
l

listen to God

God's voice is found in His word, the Bible.
Unless you have another system, read today's **change your life** Daily Bible
using Today's Date. Write in this area, any verse or verses that stand out,
touch your heart, encourage or correct you. **What is God saying to you today?**

_____

_____

_____

_____

_____

change
your
life
daily

date _____

m
e
n
t
a
l

detail your day

appointments

quiet time	☐
work out	☐
	☐
	☐
	☐
	☐
	☐
	☐
	☐
	☐
	☐
	☐
	☐
	☐
	☐
	☐

calls to make   *phone #*

letters to write/fax/email
       w   f   e
☐ ☐ ☐
☐ ☐ ☐
☐ ☐ ☐
☐ ☐ ☐

things to do

☐
☐
☐
☐
☐

define your dream

What is one practical step you can take toward reaching a goal -
and fulfilling a dream - in one or more areas of your life?

Use this space to brainstorm or to develop a dream that won't go away!

physical	emotional
mental	spiritual

change
your
life
daily

date _____

eat right

- · understand your own body type, genetics, metabolism, etc.
- · design a healthy, "plan ahead" eating plan that includes a balance
    of all the food groups in moderate portions
- · **record your daily intentions for meals and snacks below**
- · **review your progress and make daily adjustments**

breakfast	
lunch	
dinner	
snacks	

exercise regularly

- · determine what type of activity, where, when, how often and with whom you
    most like to exercise
- · develop a "week at a glance" exercise plan that includes a variety of 3 to 4 activities
    and has provision for alternate dates and times.

Detail your week plan; highlight today's plan.... what? when? where? with whom?

sun	mon	tue	wed	thur	fri	sat

journal

**Journal below about any temptations, circumstances or emotions – today --
that might keep you from reaching your goals?** (ex: vacation, celebrations, etc)

_____

_____

_____

_____

_____

_____

p
h
y
s
i
c
a
l

change
your
life
daily

date _____

e
m
o
t
i
o
n
a
l

forgive

To experience emotional balance on a daily basis, allow one or more of the below questions to prompt you to journal about the relationships in your life that need to heal and be healed.

Today, I know I need to ask _____ **to forgive me.**

I need to forgive myself for _____

I need to forgive _____ **for** _____

And I ask God to forgive me for _____

_____

_____

_____

_____

_____

_____

_____

What additional step(s) can I take to complete the healing that I have just journaled about in the above space? (ex: a phone call, letter, apology,etc.)

_____

_____

_____

_____

give

The gift of time, money, resources, or talent to an organization or person is both a powerful and practical way to help others.
What need comes to my mind -- today -- that I can find and fill and/or what person or organization needs a specific source of comfort or encouragement that I can give?

_____

_____

_____

_____

_____

change
your
life
daily

_____

date _____

talk to God

Today, in honest transparency, share -- in writing – your thoughts,
gratitude, regrets, fears, plans, hopes, dreams and requests
for yourself and others with the living, loving God.

_____
_____
_____
_____
_____
_____
_____
_____
_____
_____
_____
_____
_____
_____
_____
_____
_____
_____

s
p
i
r
i
t
u
a
l

listen to God

God's voice is found in His word, the Bible.
Unless you have another system, read today's **change your life Daily Bible**
using Today's Date. Write in this area, any verse or verses that stand out,
touch your heart, encourage or correct you. **What is God saying to you today?**

_____
_____
_____
_____
_____
_____

change
your
life
daily

date _____

m
e
n
t
a
l

detail your day

appointments

- [ ] quiet time
- [ ] work out
- [ ] _____
- [ ] _____
- [ ] _____
- [ ] _____
- [ ] _____
- [ ] _____
- [ ] _____
- [ ] _____
- [ ] _____
- [ ] _____
- [ ] _____
- [ ] _____
- [ ] _____
- [ ] _____
- [ ] _____
- [ ] _____

calls to make   *phone #*

_____

_____

_____

_____

_____

letters to write/fax/email
w   f   e

_____ [ ] [ ] [ ]

_____ [ ] [ ] [ ]

_____ [ ] [ ] [ ]

_____ [ ] [ ] [ ]

things to do

_____ [ ]

_____ [ ]

_____ [ ]

_____ [ ]

_____ [ ]

define your dream

What is one practical step you can take toward reaching a goal -
and fulfilling a dream - in one or more areas of your life?
Use this space to brainstorm or to develop a dream that won't go away!

physical | emotional
mental | spiritual

change
your
life
daily

date _____

eat right

· understand your own body type, genetics, metabolism, etc.
· design a healthy, "plan ahead" eating plan that includes a balance
  of all the food groups in moderate portions
· **record your daily intentions for meals and snacks below**
· **review your progress and make daily adjustments**

breakfast
_____

lunch
_____

dinner
_____

snacks
_____

exercise regularly

· determine what type of activity, where, when, how often and with whom you
  most like to exercise
· develop a "week at a glance" exercise plan that includes a variety of 3 to 4 activities
  and has provision for alternate dates and times.

Detail your week plan; highlight today's plan.... what? when? where? with whom?

sun	mon	tue	wed	thur	fri	sat

journal

**Journal below about any temptations, circumstances or emotions – today --
that might keep you from reaching your goals?** (ex: vacation, celebrations, etc)

_____

_____

_____

_____

_____

_____

p
h
y
s
i
c
a
l

change
your
life
daily

date _____

e
m
o
t
i
o
n
a
l

forgive

To experience emotional balance on a daily basis, allow one or more of the below questions to prompt you to journal about the relationships in your life that need to heal and be healed.

Today, I know I need to ask _____ **to forgive me.**

I need to forgive myself for _____

I need to forgive _____ **for** _____

And I ask God to forgive me for _____

_____

_____

_____

_____

_____

_____

_____

What additional step(s) can I take to complete the healing that I have just journaled about in the above space? (ex: a phone call, letter, apology,etc.)

_____

_____

_____

_____

give

The gift of time, money, resources, or talent to an organization or person is both a powerful and practical way to help others.
What need comes to my mind -- today -- that I can find and fill and/or what person or organization needs a specific source of comfort or encouragement that I can give?

_____

_____

_____

_____

_____

change
your
life
daily

_____

date _____

talk to God

Today, in honest transparency, share -- in writing – your thoughts, gratitude, regrets, fears, plans, hopes, dreams and requests for yourself and others with the living, loving God.

s
p
i
r
i
t
u
a
l

_____
_____
_____
_____
_____
_____
_____
_____
_____
_____
_____
_____
_____
_____
_____
_____
_____
_____
_____
_____

listen to God

God's voice is found in His word, the Bible.
Unless you have another system, read today's **change your life Daily Bible** using Today's Date. Write in this area, any verse or verses that stand out, touch your heart, encourage or correct you. **What is God saying to you today?**

_____
_____
_____
_____
_____
_____

change
your
life
daily

date _____

m
e
n
t
a
l

detail your day

appointments

- quiet time ☐
- work out ☐
- _____ ☐
- _____ ☐
- _____ ☐
- _____ ☐
- _____ ☐
- _____ ☐
- _____ ☐
- _____ ☐
- _____ ☐
- _____ ☐
- _____ ☐
- _____ ☐
- _____ ☐
- _____ ☐
- _____ ☐

calls to make   *phone #*

_____
_____
_____
_____
_____
_____

letters to write/fax/email
w   f   e
_____ ☐ ☐ ☐
_____ ☐ ☐ ☐
_____ ☐ ☐ ☐
_____ ☐ ☐ ☐

things to do

_____ ☐
_____ ☐
_____ ☐
_____ ☐
_____ ☐

define your dream

What is one practical step you can take toward reaching a goal -
and fulfilling a dream - in one or more areas of your life?
Use this space to brainstorm or to develop a dream that won't go away!

physical | emotional
mental | spiritual

change
your
life
daily

date _____

eat right

· understand your own body type, genetics, metabolism, etc.
· design a healthy, "plan ahead" eating plan that includes a balance
   of all the food groups in moderate portions
· **record your daily intentions for meals and snacks below**
· **review your progress and make daily adjustments**

breakfast	
lunch	
dinner	
snacks	

exercise regularly

· determine what type of activity, where, when, how often and with whom you
   most like to exercise
· develop a "week at a glance" exercise plan that includes a variety of 3 to 4 activities
   and has provision for alternate dates and times.

Detail your week plan; highlight today's plan.... what? when? where? with whom?

sun	mon	tue	wed	thur	fri	sat

journal

**Journal below about any temptations, circumstances or emotions – today --
that might keep you from reaching your goals?** (ex: vacation, celebrations, etc)

_____
_____
_____
_____
_____
_____

p
h
y
s
i
c
a
l

change
your
life
daily

date _____

e
m
o
t
i
o
n
a
l

forgive

To experience emotional balance on a daily basis, allow one or more of the below questions to prompt you to journal about the relationships in your life that need to heal and be healed.

Today, I know I need to ask _____ **to forgive me.**

I need to forgive myself for _____

I need to forgive _____ **for** _____

And I ask God to forgive me for _____

_____

_____

_____

_____

_____

_____

What additional step(s) can I take to complete the healing that I have just journaled about in the above space? (ex: a phone call, letter, apology,etc.)

_____

_____

_____

_____

give

The gift of time, money, resources, or talent to an organization or person is both a powerful and practical way to help others.
What need comes to my mind -- today -- that I can find and fill and/or what person or organization needs a specific source of comfort or encouragement that I can give?

_____

_____

_____

_____

_____

change
your
life
daily

date _____

talk to God

Today, in honest transparency, share -- in writing – your thoughts, gratitude, regrets, fears, plans, hopes, dreams and requests for yourself and others with the living, loving God.

s
p
i
r
i
t
u
a
l

_____
_____
_____
_____
_____
_____
_____
_____
_____
_____
_____
_____
_____
_____
_____
_____
_____
_____
_____
_____

listen to God

God's voice is found in His word, the Bible.
Unless you have another system, read today's **change your life Daily Bible** using Today's Date. Write in this area, any verse or verses that stand out, touch your heart, encourage or correct you. **What is God saying to you today?**

_____
_____
_____
_____
_____
_____

change
your
life
daily

date _____

m
e
n
t
a
l

detail your day

appointments

quiet time	☐
work out	☐
	☐
	☐
	☐
	☐
	☐
	☐
	☐
	☐
	☐
	☐
	☐
	☐
	☐
	☐

calls to make   *phone #*

_____

_____

_____

_____

_____

letters to write/fax/email
                                   w   f   e
                                   ☐   ☐   ☐

                                   ☐   ☐   ☐

                                   ☐   ☐   ☐

                                   ☐   ☐   ☐

things to do

_____	☐
_____	☐
_____	☐
_____	☐
_____	☐

define your dream

What is one practical step you can take toward reaching a goal -
and fulfilling a dream - in one or more areas of your life?
Use this space to brainstorm or to develop a dream that won't go away!

physical | emotional

mental | spiritual

change
your
life
daily

eat right

- · understand your own body type, genetics, metabolism, etc.
- · design a healthy, "plan ahead" eating plan that includes a balance of all the food groups in moderate portions
- · **record your daily intentions for meals and snacks below**
- · **review your progress and make daily adjustments**

breakfast _____

_____

lunch _____

_____

dinner _____

_____

snacks

exercise regularly

- · determine what type of activity, where, when, how often and with whom you most like to exercise
- · develop a "week at a glance" exercise plan that includes a variety of 3 to 4 activities and has provision for alternate dates and times.

Detail your week plan; highlight today's plan.... what? when? where? with whom?

sun	mon	tue	wed	thur	fri	sat

journal

Journal below about any temptations, circumstances or emotions – today -- that might keep you from reaching your goals? (ex: vacation, celebrations, etc)

_____

_____

_____

_____

_____

_____

p
h
y
s
i
c
a
l

change
your
life
daily

date _____

e
m
o
t
i
o
n
a
l

forgive

To experience emotional balance on a daily basis, allow one or more of the below questions to prompt you to journal about the relationships in your life that need to heal and be healed.

Today, I know I need to ask _____ **to forgive me.**

I need to forgive myself for _____

I need to forgive _____ **for** _____

And I ask God to forgive me for _____

_____

_____

_____

_____

_____

_____

What additional step(s) can I take to complete the healing that I have just journaled about in the above space? (ex: a phone call, letter, apology,etc.)

_____

_____

_____

give

The gift of time, money, resources, or talent to an organization or person is both a powerful and practical way to help others.
What need comes to my mind -- today -- that I can find and fill and/or what person or organization needs a specific source of comfort or encouragement that I can give?

_____

_____

_____

_____

_____

change
your
life
daily

date _____

talk to God

Today, in honest transparency, share -- in writing – your thoughts, gratitude, regrets, fears, plans, hopes, dreams and requests for yourself and others with the living, loving God.

s
p
i
r
i
t
u
a
l

_____
_____
_____
_____
_____
_____
_____
_____
_____
_____
_____
_____
_____
_____
_____
_____
_____
_____

listen to God

God's voice is found in His word, the Bible.
Unless you have another system, read today's **change your life Daily Bible** using Today's Date. Write in this area, any verse or verses that stand out, touch your heart, encourage or correct you. **What is God saying to you today?**

_____
_____
_____
_____
_____
_____

change
your
life
daily

date _____

m
e
n
t
a
l

detail your day

appointments

quiet time ☐
work out ☐
_____ ☐
_____ ☐
_____ ☐
_____ ☐
_____ ☐
_____ ☐
_____ ☐
_____ ☐
_____ ☐
_____ ☐
_____ ☐
_____ ☐
_____ ☐
_____ ☐

calls to make   *phone #*

_____
_____
_____
_____
_____

letters to write/fax/email
                          w   f   e
_____ ☐ ☐ ☐
_____ ☐ ☐ ☐
_____ ☐ ☐ ☐
_____ ☐ ☐ ☐

things to do

_____ ☐
_____ ☐
_____ ☐
_____ ☐
_____ ☐

define your dream

What is one practical step you can take toward reaching a goal -
and fulfilling a dream - in one or more areas of your life?
Use this space to brainstorm or to develop a dream that won't go away!

physical | emotional
mental | spiritual

change
your
life
daily

date _____

eat right

- · understand your own body type, genetics, metabolism, etc.
- · design a healthy, "plan ahead" eating plan that includes a balance of all the food groups in moderate portions
- · **record your daily intentions for meals and snacks below**
- · **review your progress and make daily adjustments**

breakfast	
lunch	
dinner	
snacks	

exercise regularly

- · determine what type of activity, where, when, how often and with whom you most like to exercise
- · develop a "week at a glance" exercise plan that includes a variety of 3 to 4 activities and has provision for alternate dates and times.

Detail your week plan; highlight today's plan.... what? when? where? with whom?

sun	mon	tue	wed	thur	fri	sat

journal

Journal below about any temptations, circumstances or emotions – today -- that might keep you from reaching your goals? (ex: vacation, celebrations, etc)

_____

_____

_____

_____

_____

p
h
y
s
i
c
a
l

change
your
life
daily

date _____

e
m
o
t
i
o
n
a
l

forgive

To experience emotional balance on a daily basis, allow one or more of the below questions to prompt you to journal about the relationships in your life that need to heal and be healed.

Today, I know I need to ask _____ **to forgive me.**

I need to forgive myself for _____

I need to forgive _____ **for** _____

And I ask God to forgive me for _____

_____

_____

_____

_____

_____

_____

What additional step(s) can I take to complete the healing that I have just journaled about in the above space? (ex: a phone call, letter, apology,etc.)

_____

_____

_____

_____

give

The gift of time, money, resources, or talent to an organization or person is both a powerful and practical way to help others.
What need comes to my mind -- today -- that I can find and fill and/or what person or organization needs a specific source of comfort or encouragement that I can give?

_____

_____

_____

_____

_____

_____

change
your
life
daily

date _____

talk to God

Today, in honest transparency, share -- in writing – your thoughts, gratitude, regrets, fears, plans, hopes, dreams and requests for yourself and others with the living, loving God.

s
p
i
r
i
t
u
a
l

_____

_____

_____

_____

_____

_____

_____

_____

_____

_____

_____

_____

_____

_____

_____

_____

_____

_____

_____

_____

listen to God

God's voice is found in His word, the Bible.
Unless you have another system, read today's **change your life Daily Bible** using Today's Date. Write in this area, any verse or verses that stand out, touch your heart, encourage or correct you. **What is God saying to you today?**

_____

_____

_____

_____

_____

_____

change
your
life
daily

date _____

m
e
n
t
a
l

detail your day

appointments

quiet time	☐
work out	☐
	☐
	☐
	☐
	☐
	☐
	☐
	☐
	☐
	☐
	☐
	☐
	☐
	☐
	☐

calls to make   *phone #*

letters to write/fax/email
w   f   e
☐ ☐ ☐
☐ ☐ ☐
☐ ☐ ☐
☐ ☐ ☐

things to do

☐
☐
☐
☐
☐

define your dream

What is one practical step you can take toward reaching a goal -
and fulfilling a dream - in one or more areas of your life?
Use this space to brainstorm or to develop a dream that won't go away!

physical	emotional
mental	spiritual

change
your
life
daily

date _____

eat right

- understand your own body type, genetics, metabolism, etc.
- design a healthy, "plan ahead" eating plan that includes a balance of all the food groups in moderate portions
- **record your daily intentions for meals and snacks below**
- **review your progress and make daily adjustments**

breakfast	
lunch	
dinner	
snacks	

exercise regularly

- determine what type of activity, where, when, how often and with whom you most like to exercise
- develop a "week at a glance" exercise plan that includes a variety of 3 to 4 activities and has provision for alternate dates and times.

Detail your week plan; highlight today's plan.... what? when? where? with whom?

sun	mon	tue	wed	thur	fri	sat

journal

Journal below about any temptations, circumstances or emotions – today -- that might keep you from reaching your goals? (ex: vacation, celebrations, etc)

_____

_____

_____

_____

_____

_____

physical

change
your
life
daily

date _____

e m o t i o n a l

forgive

To experience emotional balance on a daily basis, allow one or more of the below questions to prompt you to journal about the relationships in your life that need to heal and be healed.

Today, I know I need to ask _____ **to forgive me.**

I need to forgive myself for _____

I need to forgive _____ **for** _____

And I ask God to forgive me for _____

_____

_____

_____

_____

_____

_____

What additional step(s) can I take to complete the healing that I have just journaled about in the above space? (ex: a phone call, letter, apology, etc.)

_____

_____

_____

give

The gift of time, money, resources, or talent to an organization or person is both a powerful and practical way to help others.
What need comes to my mind -- today -- that I can find and fill and/or what person or organization needs a specific source of comfort or encouragement that I can give?

_____

_____

_____

_____

change
your
life
daily

date _____

talk to God

Today, in honest transparency, share -- in writing – your thoughts, gratitude, regrets, fears, plans, hopes, dreams and requests for yourself and others with the living, loving God.

s
p
i
r
i
t
u
a
l

_____
_____
_____
_____
_____
_____
_____
_____
_____
_____
_____
_____
_____
_____
_____
_____
_____
_____
_____

listen to God

God's voice is found in His word, the Bible.
Unless you have another system, read today's **change your life** **Daily Bible**
using Today's Date. Write in this area, any verse or verses that stand out,
touch your heart, encourage or correct you. **What is God saying to you today?**

_____
_____
_____
_____
_____

change
your
life
daily

date _____

m
e
n
t
a
l

detail your day

appointments

- quiet time ☐
- work out ☐
- _____ ☐
- _____ ☐
- _____ ☐
- _____ ☐
- _____ ☐
- _____ ☐
- _____ ☐
- _____ ☐
- _____ ☐
- _____ ☐
- _____ ☐
- _____ ☐
- _____ ☐
- _____ ☐

calls to make   _phone #_

_____
_____
_____
_____
_____

letters to write/fax/email
                              _w   f   e_
_____ ☐ ☐ ☐
_____ ☐ ☐ ☐
_____ ☐ ☐ ☐
_____ ☐ ☐ ☐

things to do

_____ ☐
_____ ☐
_____ ☐
_____ ☐
_____ ☐

define your dream

What is one practical step you can take toward reaching a goal -
and fulfilling a dream - in one or more areas of your life?
Use this space to brainstorm or to develop a dream that won't go away!

physical | emotional
mental | spiritual

change
your
life
daily

date _____

eat right

- understand your own body type, genetics, metabolism, etc.
- design a healthy, "plan ahead" eating plan that includes a balance of all the food groups in moderate portions
- **record your daily intentions for meals and snacks below**
- **review your progress and make daily adjustments**

breakfast _____

lunch _____

dinner _____

snacks _____

exercise regularly

- determine what type of activity, where, when, how often and with whom you most like to exercise
- develop a "week at a glance" exercise plan that includes a variety of 3 to 4 activities and has provision for alternate dates and times.

Detail your week plan; highlight today's plan.... what? when? where? with whom?

sun	mon	tue	wed	thur	fri	sat

journal

Journal below about any temptations, circumstances or emotions – today -- that might keep you from reaching your goals? (ex: vacation, celebrations, etc)

_____

_____

_____

_____

_____

_____

p h y s i c a l

change your life daily

date _____

e
m
o
t
i
o
n
a
l

forgive

To experience emotional balance on a daily basis, allow one or more of the below questions to prompt you to journal about the relationships in your life that need to heal and be healed.

Today, I know I need to ask _____ **to forgive me.**

I need to forgive myself for _____

I need to forgive _____ **for** _____

And I ask God to forgive me for _____

_____

_____

_____

_____

_____

_____

What additional step(s) can I take to complete the healing that I have just journaled about in the above space? (ex: a phone call, letter, apology,etc.)

_____

_____

_____

_____

give

The gift of time, money, resources, or talent to an organization or person is both a powerful and practical way to help others.
What need comes to my mind -- today -- that I can find and fill and/or what person or organization needs a specific source of comfort or encouragement that I can give?

_____

_____

_____

_____

_____

change
your
life
daily

talk to God

Today, in honest transparency, share -- in writing – your thoughts, gratitude, regrets, fears, plans, hopes, dreams and requests for yourself and others with the living, loving God.

s
p
i
r
i
t
u
a
l

_____

_____

_____

_____

_____

_____

_____

_____

_____

_____

_____

_____

_____

_____

_____

_____

_____

_____

listen to God

God's voice is found in His word, the Bible.
Unless you have another system, read today's **change your life Daily Bible** using Today's Date. Write in this area, any verse or verses that stand out, touch your heart, encourage or correct you. **What is God saying to you today?**

_____

_____

_____

_____

_____

_____

change
your
life
daily

date _____

m
e
n
t
a
l

detail your day

appointments

quiet time ☐
work out ☐
_____ ☐
_____ ☐
_____ ☐
_____ ☐
_____ ☐
_____ ☐
_____ ☐
_____ ☐
_____ ☐
_____ ☐
_____ ☐
_____ ☐
_____ ☐
_____ ☐
_____ ☐

calls to make   *phone #*

_____
_____
_____
_____
_____
_____

letters to write/fax/email
          w   f   e
_____ ☐ ☐ ☐
_____ ☐ ☐ ☐
_____ ☐ ☐ ☐
_____ ☐ ☐ ☐

things to do

_____ ☐
_____ ☐
_____ ☐
_____ ☐
_____ ☐

define your dream

What is one practical step you can take toward reaching a goal -
and fulfilling a dream - in one or more areas of your life?
Use this space to brainstorm or to develop a dream that won't go away!

physical | emotional
mental | spiritual

change
your
life
daily

date _____

eat right

- understand your own body type, genetics, metabolism, etc.
- design a healthy, "plan ahead" eating plan that includes a balance of all the food groups in moderate portions
- **record your daily intentions for meals and snacks below**
- **review your progress and make daily adjustments**

p
h
y
s
i
c
a
l

breakfast	
lunch	
dinner	
snacks	

exercise regularly

- determine what type of activity, where, when, how often and with whom you most like to exercise
- develop a "week at a glance" exercise plan that includes a variety of 3 to 4 activities and has provision for alternate dates and times.

Detail your week plan; highlight today's plan.... what? when? where? with whom?

sun	mon	tue	wed	thur	fri	sat

journal

Journal below about any temptations, circumstances or emotions – today -- that might keep you from reaching your goals? (ex: vacation, celebrations, etc)

_____

_____

_____

_____

_____

_____

change
your
life
daily

date _____

e
m
o
t
i
o
n
a
l

forgive

To experience emotional balance on a daily basis, allow one or more of the below questions to prompt you to journal about the relationships in your life that need to heal and be healed.

Today, I know I need to ask _____ **to forgive me.**

I need to forgive myself for _____

I need to forgive _____ **for** _____

And I ask God to forgive me for _____

_____

_____

_____

_____

_____

_____

What additional step(s) can I take to complete the healing that I have just journaled about in the above space? (ex: a phone call, letter, apology, etc.)

_____

_____

_____

_____

give

The gift of time, money, resources, or talent to an organization or person is both a powerful and practical way to help others.
What need comes to my mind -- today -- that I can find and fill and/or what person or organization needs a specific source of comfort or encouragement that I can give?

_____

_____

_____

_____

_____

change
your
life
daily

date _____

talk to God

Today, in honest transparency, share -- in writing – your thoughts, gratitude, regrets, fears, plans, hopes, dreams and requests for yourself and others with the living, loving God.

s
p
i
r
i
t
u
a
l

_____

_____

_____

_____

_____

_____

_____

_____

_____

_____

_____

_____

_____

_____

_____

_____

_____

listen to God

God's voice is found in His word, the Bible.
Unless you have another system, read today's **change your life Daily Bible** using Today's Date. Write in this area, any verse or verses that stand out, touch your heart, encourage or correct you. **What is God saying to you today?**

_____

_____

_____

_____

_____

_____

change
your
life
daily

date _____

m e n t a l

detail your day

appointments

- quiet time ☐
- work out ☐
- _____ ☐
- _____ ☐
- _____ ☐
- _____ ☐
- _____ ☐
- _____ ☐
- _____ ☐
- _____ ☐
- _____ ☐
- _____ ☐
- _____ ☐
- _____ ☐
- _____ ☐
- _____ ☐
- _____ ☐

calls to make   *phone #*

- _____
- _____
- _____
- _____
- _____

letters to write/fax/email
w   f   e

- _____ ☐ ☐ ☐
- _____ ☐ ☐ ☐
- _____ ☐ ☐ ☐
- _____ ☐ ☐ ☐

things to do

- _____ ☐
- _____ ☐
- _____ ☐
- _____ ☐
- _____ ☐

define your dream

What is one practical step you can take toward reaching a goal -
and fulfilling a dream - in one or more areas of your life?
Use this space to brainstorm or to develop a dream that won't go away!

physical | emotional

mental | spiritual

change

your

life

daily

date _____

eat right

- · understand your own body type, genetics, metabolism, etc.
- · design a healthy, "plan ahead" eating plan that includes a balance of all the food groups in moderate portions
- **· record your daily intentions for meals and snacks below**
- **· review your progress and make daily adjustments**

p
h
y
s
i
c
a
l

breakfast _____

lunch _____

dinner _____

snacks _____

exercise regularly

- · determine what type of activity, where, when, how often and with whom you most like to exercise
- · develop a "week at a glance" exercise plan that includes a variety of 3 to 4 activities and has provision for alternate dates and times.

Detail your week plan; highlight today's plan.... what? when? where? with whom?

sun	mon	tue	wed	thur	fri	sat

journal

Journal below about any temptations, circumstances or emotions – today -- that might keep you from reaching your goals? (ex: vacation, celebrations, etc)

_____

_____

_____

_____

_____

_____

change
your
life
daily

date _____

forgive

To experience emotional balance on a daily basis, allow one or more of the below questions to prompt you to journal about the relationships in your life that need to heal and be healed.

Today, I know I need to ask _____ **to forgive me.**

I need to forgive myself for _____

I need to forgive _____ **for** _____

And I ask God to forgive me for _____

_____

_____

_____

_____

_____

_____

What additional step(s) can I take to complete the healing that I have just journaled about in the above space? (ex: a phone call, letter, apology, etc.)

_____

_____

_____

give

The gift of time, money, resources, or talent to an organization or person is both a powerful and practical way to help others.
What need comes to my mind -- today -- that I can find and fill and/or what person or organization needs a specific source of comfort or encouragement that I can give?

_____

_____

_____

_____

_____

date _____

talk to God

Today, in honest transparency, share -- in writing – your thoughts, gratitude, regrets, fears, plans, hopes, dreams and requests for yourself and others with the living, loving God.

s
p
i
r
i
t
u
a
l

_____

_____

_____

_____

_____

_____

_____

_____

_____

_____

_____

_____

_____

_____

_____

_____

_____

_____

listen to God

God's voice is found in His word, the Bible.
Unless you have another system, read today's **change your life** **Daily Bible**
using Today's Date. Write in this area, any verse or verses that stand out,
touch your heart, encourage or correct you. **What is God saying to you today?**

_____

_____

_____

_____

_____

_____

change
your
life
daily

date _____

m
e
n
t
a
l

detail your day

appointments

quiet time ☐
work out ☐
_____ ☐
_____ ☐
_____ ☐
_____ ☐
_____ ☐
_____ ☐
_____ ☐
_____ ☐
_____ ☐
_____ ☐
_____ ☐
_____ ☐
_____ ☐
_____ ☐

calls to make   *phone #*

_____
_____
_____
_____
_____
_____

letters to write/fax/email
w   f   e
☐ ☐ ☐
_____
☐ ☐ ☐
_____
☐ ☐ ☐
_____
☐ ☐ ☐

things to do

_____ ☐
_____ ☐
_____ ☐
_____ ☐
_____ ☐

define your dream

What is one practical step you can take toward reaching a goal -
and fulfilling a dream - in one or more areas of your life?
Use this space to brainstorm or to develop a dream that won't go away!

physical | emotional
mental | spiritual

change
your
life
daily

date _____

eat right

- understand your own body type, genetics, metabolism, etc.
- design a healthy, "plan ahead" eating plan that includes a balance of all the food groups in moderate portions
- **record your daily intentions for meals and snacks below**
- **review your progress and make daily adjustments**

breakfast	
lunch	
dinner	
snacks	

exercise regularly

- determine what type of activity, where, when, how often and with whom you most like to exercise
- develop a "week at a glance" exercise plan that includes a variety of 3 to 4 activities and has provision for alternate dates and times.

Detail your week plan; highlight today's plan.... what? when? where? with whom?

sun	mon	tue	wed	thur	fri	sat

journal

Journal below about any temptations, circumstances or emotions – today -- that might keep you from reaching your goals? (ex: vacation, celebrations, etc)

_____

_____

_____

_____

_____

_____

p
h
y
s
i
c
a
l

change
your
life
daily

date _____

e
m
o
t
i
o
n
a
l

forgive

To experience emotional balance on a daily basis, allow one or more of the below questions to prompt you to journal about the relationships in your life that need to heal and be healed.

Today, I know I need to ask _____ **to forgive me.**

I need to forgive myself for _____

I need to forgive _____ **for** _____

And I ask God to forgive me for _____

_____

_____

_____

_____

_____

_____

_____

What additional step(s) can I take to complete the healing that I have just journaled about in the above space? (ex: a phone call, letter, apology,etc.)

_____

_____

_____

give

The gift of time, money, resources, or talent to an organization or person is both a powerful and practical way to help others.
What need comes to my mind -- today -- that I can find and fill and/or what person or organization needs a specific source of comfort or encouragement that I can give?

_____

_____

_____

_____

_____

change
your
life
daily

date _____

talk to God

Today, in honest transparency, share -- in writing – your thoughts, gratitude, regrets, fears, plans, hopes, dreams and requests for yourself and others with the living, loving God.

s
p
i
r
i
t
u
a
l

_____
_____
_____
_____
_____
_____
_____
_____
_____
_____
_____
_____
_____
_____
_____
_____
_____
_____
_____

listen to God

God's voice is found in His word, the Bible.
Unless you have another system, read today's **change your life Daily Bible**
using Today's Date. Write in this area, any verse or verses that stand out,
touch your heart, encourage or correct you. **What is God saying to you today?**

_____
_____
_____
_____
_____
_____

change
your
life
daily

date _____

m
e
n
t
a
l

detail your day

appointments

quiet time ☐
work out ☐
_____ ☐
_____ ☐
_____ ☐
_____ ☐
_____ ☐
_____ ☐
_____ ☐
_____ ☐
_____ ☐
_____ ☐
_____ ☐
_____ ☐
_____ ☐
_____ ☐
_____ ☐

calls to make   *phone #*

_____
_____
_____
_____
_____

letters to write/fax/email
w   f   e

_____ ☐ ☐ ☐
_____ ☐ ☐ ☐
_____ ☐ ☐ ☐
_____ ☐ ☐ ☐

things to do

_____ ☐
_____ ☐
_____ ☐
_____ ☐
_____ ☐

define your dream

What is one practical step you can take toward reaching a goal -
and fulfilling a dream - in one or more areas of your life?
Use this space to brainstorm or to develop a dream that won't go away!

physical | emotional
mental | spiritual

change
your
life
daily

date _____

eat right

- · understand your own body type, genetics, metabolism, etc.
- · design a healthy, "plan ahead" eating plan that includes a balance of all the food groups in moderate portions
- · **record your daily intentions for meals and snacks below**
- · **review your progress and make daily adjustments**

breakfast	
lunch	
dinner	
snacks	

exercise regularly

- · determine what type of activity, where, when, how often and with whom you most like to exercise
- · develop a "week at a glance" exercise plan that includes a variety of 3 to 4 activities and has provision for alternate dates and times.

Detail your week plan; highlight today's plan.... what? when? where? with whom?

sun	mon	tue	wed	thur	fri	sat

journal

Journal below about any temptations, circumstances or emotions – today -- that might keep you from reaching your goals? (ex: vacation, celebrations, etc)

_____

_____

_____

_____

_____

_____

p
h
y
s
i
c
a
l

change
your
life
daily

date _____

e
m
o
t
i
o
n
a
l

forgive

To experience emotional balance on a daily basis, allow one or more of the below questions to prompt you to journal about the relationships in your life that need to heal and be healed.

Today, I know I need to ask _____ **to forgive me.**

I need to forgive myself for _____

I need to forgive _____ **for** _____

And I ask God to forgive me for _____

_____

_____

_____

_____

_____

_____

What additional step(s) can I take to complete the healing that I have just journaled about in the above space? (ex: a phone call, letter, apology,etc.)

_____

_____

_____

give

The gift of time, money, resources, or talent to an organization or person is both a powerful and practical way to help others.
What need comes to my mind -- today -- that I can find and fill and/or what person or organization needs a specific source of comfort or encouragement that I can give?

_____

_____

_____

_____

_____

change
your
life
daily

date _____

talk to God

Today, in honest transparency, share -- in writing – your thoughts,
gratitude, regrets, fears, plans, hopes, dreams and requests
for yourself and others with the living, loving God.

s
p
i
r
i
t
u
a
l

_____
_____
_____
_____
_____
_____
_____
_____
_____
_____
_____
_____
_____
_____
_____
_____
_____
_____
_____

listen to God

God's voice is found in His word, the Bible.
Unless you have another system, read today's **change your life** **Daily Bible**
using Today's Date. Write in this area, any verse or verses that stand out,
touch your heart, encourage or correct you. **What is God saying to you today?**

_____
_____
_____
_____
_____
_____

change
your
life
daily

date _____

m
e
n
t
a
l

detail your day

appointments

quiet time	☐
work out	☐
	☐
	☐
	☐
	☐
	☐
	☐
	☐
	☐
	☐
	☐
	☐
	☐
	☐
	☐

calls to make   *phone #*

_____

_____

_____

_____

_____

letters to write/fax/email
w   f   e

_____ ☐ ☐ ☐

_____ ☐ ☐ ☐

_____ ☐ ☐ ☐

_____ ☐ ☐ ☐

things to do

_____ ☐

_____ ☐

_____ ☐

_____ ☐

_____ ☐

define your dream

What is one practical step you can take toward reaching a goal -
and fulfilling a dream - in one or more areas of your life?
Use this space to brainstorm or to develop a dream that won't go away!

physical	emotional
mental	spiritual

change
your
life
daily

date _____

eat right

- understand your own body type, genetics, metabolism, etc.
- design a healthy, "plan ahead" eating plan that includes a balance of all the food groups in moderate portions
- **record your daily intentions for meals and snacks below**
- **review your progress and make daily adjustments**

breakfast	
lunch	
dinner	
snacks	

exercise regularly

- determine what type of activity, where, when, how often and with whom you most like to exercise
- develop a "week at a glance" exercise plan that includes a variety of 3 to 4 activities and has provision for alternate dates and times.

Detail your week plan; highlight today's plan.... what? when? where? with whom?

| sun | mon | tue | wed | thur | fri | sat |

journal

Journal below about any temptations, circumstances or emotions – today -- that might keep you from reaching your goals? (ex: vacation, celebrations, etc)

_____

_____

_____

_____

_____

_____

p
h
y
s
i
c
a
l

change
your
life
daily

date _____

e

m

o

t

i

o

n

a

l

forgive

To experience emotional balance on a daily basis, allow one or more of the below questions to prompt you to journal about the relationships in your life that need to heal and be healed.

Today, I know I need to ask _____ **to forgive me.**

I need to forgive myself for _____

I need to forgive _____ **for** _____

And I ask God to forgive me for _____

_____

_____

_____

_____

_____

_____

_____

What additional step(s) can I take to complete the healing that I have just journaled about in the above space? (ex: a phone call, letter, apology,etc.)

_____

_____

_____

_____

give

The gift of time, money, resources, or talent to an organization or person is both a powerful and practical way to help others.
What need comes to my mind -- today -- that I can find and fill and/or what person or organization needs a specific source of comfort or encouragement that I can give?

_____

_____

_____

_____

_____

_____

change

your

life

daily

date _____

talk to God

Today, in honest transparency, share -- in writing – your thoughts, gratitude, regrets, fears, plans, hopes, dreams and requests for yourself and others with the living, loving God.

s
p
i
r
i
t
u
a
l

listen to God

God's voice is found in His word, the Bible.
Unless you have another system, read today's **change your life Daily Bible** using Today's Date. Write in this area, any verse or verses that stand out, touch your heart, encourage or correct you. **What is God saying to you today?**

change
your
life
daily

date _____

m
e
n
t
a
l

detail your day

appointments

quiet time	☐
work out	☐
	☐
	☐
	☐
	☐
	☐
	☐
	☐
	☐
	☐
	☐
	☐
	☐
	☐
	☐
	☐

calls to make   *phone #*

letters to write/fax/email
w   f   e
☐ ☐ ☐
☐ ☐ ☐
☐ ☐ ☐
☐ ☐ ☐

things to do

☐
☐
☐
☐
☐

define your dream

What is one practical step you can take toward reaching a goal -
and fulfilling a dream - in one or more areas of your life?
Use this space to brainstorm or to develop a dream that won't go away!

physical	emotional
mental	spiritual

change
your
life
daily

date _____

eat right

- · understand your own body type, genetics, metabolism, etc.
- · design a healthy, "plan ahead" eating plan that includes a balance of all the food groups in moderate portions
- · **record your daily intentions for meals and snacks below**
- · **review your progress and make daily adjustments**

breakfast	
lunch	
dinner	
snacks	

exercise regularly

- · determine what type of activity, where, when, how often and with whom you most like to exercise
- · develop a "week at a glance" exercise plan that includes a variety of 3 to 4 activities and has provision for alternate dates and times.

Detail your week plan; highlight today's plan.... what? when? where? with whom?

sun	mon	tue	wed	thur	fri	sat

journal

Journal below about any temptations, circumstances or emotions – today -- that might keep you from reaching your goals? (ex: vacation, celebrations, etc)

_____

_____

_____

_____

_____

_____

p
h
y
s
i
c
a
l

change
your
life
daily

date _____

e

m

o

t

i

o

n

a

l

forgive

To experience emotional balance on a daily basis, allow one or more of the below questions to prompt you to journal about the relationships in your life that need to heal and be healed.

Today, I know I need to ask _____ **to forgive me.**

I need to forgive myself for _____

I need to forgive _____ **for** _____

And I ask God to forgive me for _____

_____

_____

_____

_____

_____

_____

What additional step(s) can I take to complete the healing that I have just journaled about in the above space? (ex: a phone call, letter, apology,etc.)

_____

_____

_____

_____

give

The gift of time, money, resources, or talent to an organization or person is both a powerful and practical way to help others.
What need comes to my mind -- today -- that I can find and fill and/or what person or organization needs a specific source of comfort or encouragement that I can give?

_____

_____

_____

_____

_____

change

your

life

daily

date _____

talk to God

Today, in honest transparency, share -- in writing – your thoughts,
gratitude, regrets, fears, plans, hopes, dreams and requests
for yourself and others with the living, loving God.

_____

_____

_____

_____

_____

_____

_____

_____

_____

_____

_____

_____

_____

_____

_____

_____

s
p
i
r
i
t
u
a
l

listen to God

God's voice is found in His word, the Bible.
Unless you have another system, read today's **change your life** Daily Bible
using Today's Date. Write in this area, any verse or verses that stand out,
touch your heart, encourage or correct you. **What is God saying to you today?**

_____

_____

_____

_____

_____

change
your
life
daily

date _____

m
e
n
t
a
l

detail your day

appointments

quiet time ☐
work out ☐
_____ ☐
_____ ☐
_____ ☐
_____ ☐
_____ ☐
_____ ☐
_____ ☐
_____ ☐
_____ ☐
_____ ☐
_____ ☐
_____ ☐
_____ ☐
_____ ☐

calls to make   *phone #*

_____
_____
_____
_____
_____

letters to write/fax/email
w f e
_____ ☐ ☐ ☐
_____ ☐ ☐ ☐
_____ ☐ ☐ ☐
_____ ☐ ☐ ☐

things to do

_____ ☐
_____ ☐
_____ ☐
_____ ☐
_____ ☐

define your dream

What is one practical step you can take toward reaching a goal -
and fulfilling a dream - in one or more areas of your life?
Use this space to brainstorm or to develop a dream that won't go away!

physical | emotional
mental | spiritual

change
your
life
daily

date _____

eat right

- · understand your own body type, genetics, metabolism, etc.
- · design a healthy, "plan ahead" eating plan that includes a balance of all the food groups in moderate portions
- · **record your daily intentions for meals and snacks below**
- · **review your progress and make daily adjustments**

breakfast	
lunch	
dinner	
snacks	

exercise regularly

- · determine what type of activity, where, when, how often and with whom you most like to exercise
- · develop a "week at a glance" exercise plan that includes a variety of 3 to 4 activities and has provision for alternate dates and times.

Detail your week plan; highlight today's plan.... what? when? where? with whom?

sun	mon	tue	wed	thur	fri	sat

journal

Journal below about any temptations, circumstances or emotions – today -- that might keep you from reaching your goals? (ex: vacation, celebrations, etc)

_____

_____

_____

_____

_____

_____

physical

change
your
life
daily

date _____

e

m

o

t

i

o

n

a

l

forgive

To experience emotional balance on a daily basis, allow one or more of the below questions to prompt you to journal about the relationships in your life that need to heal and be healed.

Today, I know I need to ask _____ **to forgive me.**

I need to forgive myself for _____

I need to forgive _____ **for** _____

And I ask God to forgive me for _____

_____

_____

_____

_____

_____

_____

What additional step(s) can I take to complete the healing that I have just journaled about in the above space? (ex: a phone call, letter, apology, etc.)

_____

_____

_____

_____

give

The gift of time, money, resources, or talent to an organization or person is both a powerful and practical way to help others.
What need comes to my mind -- today -- that I can find and fill and/or what person or organization needs a specific source of comfort or encouragement that I can give?

_____

_____

_____

_____

_____

_____

change

your

life

daily

date _____

talk to God

**Today, in honest transparency, share -- in writing – your thoughts,
gratitude, regrets, fears, plans, hopes, dreams and requests
for yourself and others with the living, loving God.**

s
p
i
r
i
t
u
a
l

_____

_____

_____

_____

_____

_____

_____

_____

_____

_____

_____

_____

_____

_____

_____

_____

_____

_____

listen to God

God's voice is found in His word, the Bible.
Unless you have another system, read today's **change your life Daily Bible**
using Today's Date. Write in this area, any verse or verses that stand out,
touch your heart, encourage or correct you. **What is God saying to you today?**

_____

_____

_____

_____

_____

change
your
life
daily

date _____

m
e
n
t
a
l

detail your day

appointments

quiet time	☐
work out	☐
	☐
	☐
	☐
	☐
	☐
	☐
	☐
	☐
	☐
	☐
	☐
	☐
	☐
	☐
	☐

calls to make   *phone #*

letters to write/fax/email
w   f   e
☐ ☐ ☐
☐ ☐ ☐
☐ ☐ ☐
☐ ☐ ☐

things to do
☐
☐
☐
☐
☐

define your dream

What is one practical step you can take toward reaching a goal -
and fulfilling a dream - in one or more areas of your life?
Use this space to brainstorm or to develop a dream that won't go away!

physical | emotional
mental | spiritual

change
your
life
daily

date _____

eat right

- · understand your own body type, genetics, metabolism, etc.
- · design a healthy, "plan ahead" eating plan that includes a balance of all the food groups in moderate portions
- · **record your daily intentions for meals and snacks below**
- · **review your progress and make daily adjustments**

breakfast
_____

lunch
_____

dinner
_____

snacks
_____

exercise regularly

- · determine what type of activity, where, when, how often and with whom you most like to exercise
- · develop a "week at a glance" exercise plan that includes a variety of 3 to 4 activities and has provision for alternate dates and times.

Detail your week plan; highlight today's plan.... what? when? where? with whom?

sun	mon	tue	wed	thur	fri	sat

journal

Journal below about any temptations, circumstances or emotions – today -- that might keep you from reaching your goals? (ex: vacation, celebrations, etc)

_____

_____

_____

_____

_____

p
h
y
s
i
c
a
l

change
your
life
daily

date _____

e
m
o
t
i
o
n
a
l

forgive

To experience emotional balance on a daily basis, allow one or more of the below questions to prompt you to journal about the relationships in your life that need to heal and be healed.

Today, I know I need to ask _____ **to forgive me.**

I need to forgive myself for _____

I need to forgive _____ **for** _____

And I ask God to forgive me for _____

_____

_____

_____

_____

_____

_____

What additional step(s) can I take to complete the healing that I have just journaled about in the above space? (ex: a phone call, letter, apology,etc.)

_____

_____

_____

_____

give

The gift of time, money, resources, or talent to an organization or person is both a powerful and practical way to help others.
What need comes to my mind -- today -- that I can find and fill and/or what person or organization needs a specific source of comfort or encouragement that I can give?

_____

_____

_____

_____

_____

_____

change
your
life
daily

date _____

talk to God

Today, in honest transparency, share -- in writing – your thoughts,
gratitude, regrets, fears, plans, hopes, dreams and requests
for yourself and others with the living, loving God.

s
p
i
r
i
t
u
a
l

_____

_____

_____

_____

_____

_____

_____

_____

_____

_____

_____

_____

_____

_____

_____

_____

_____

_____

_____

listen to God

God's voice is found in His word, the Bible.
Unless you have another system, read today's **change your life** Daily Bible
using Today's Date. Write in this area, any verse or verses that stand out,
touch your heart, encourage or correct you. **What is God saying to you today?**

_____

_____

_____

_____

_____

_____

change
your
life
daily

date _____

m e n t a l

detail your day

appointments

quiet time ☐

work out ☐

_____ ☐

_____ ☐

_____ ☐

_____ ☐

_____ ☐

_____ ☐

_____ ☐

_____ ☐

_____ ☐

_____ ☐

_____ ☐

_____ ☐

_____ ☐

_____ ☐

_____ ☐

calls to make   *phone #*

_____

_____

_____

_____

_____

letters to write/fax/email
w   f   e
☐ ☐ ☐

_____ ☐ ☐ ☐

_____ ☐ ☐ ☐

_____ ☐ ☐ ☐

_____ ☐ ☐ ☐

things to do

_____ ☐

_____ ☐

_____ ☐

_____ ☐

_____ ☐

define your dream

What is one practical step you can take toward reaching a goal -
and fulfilling a dream - in one or more areas of your life?
Use this space to brainstorm or to develop a dream that won't go away!

physical | emotional

mental | spiritual

change
your
life
daily

date _____

eat right

- · understand your own body type, genetics, metabolism, etc.
- · design a healthy, "plan ahead" eating plan that includes a balance of all the food groups in moderate portions
- · **record your daily intentions for meals and snacks below**
- · **review your progress and make daily adjustments**

p
h
y
s
i
c
a
l

breakfast	
lunch	
dinner	
snacks	

exercise regularly

- · determine what type of activity, where, when, how often and with whom you most like to exercise
- · develop a "week at a glance" exercise plan that includes a variety of 3 to 4 activities and has provision for alternate dates and times.

Detail your week plan; highlight today's plan.... what? when? where? with whom?

sun	mon	tue	wed	thur	fri	sat

journal

Journal below about any temptations, circumstances or emotions – today -- that might keep you from reaching your goals? (ex: vacation, celebrations, etc)

_____

_____

_____

_____

_____

_____

change
your
life
daily

date _____

e

m

o

t

i

o

n

a

l

forgive

To experience emotional balance on a daily basis, allow one or more of the below questions to prompt you to journal about the relationships in your life that need to heal and be healed.

Today, I know I need to ask _____ **to forgive me.**

I need to forgive myself for _____

I need to forgive _____ **for** _____

And I ask God to forgive me for _____

_____

_____

_____

_____

_____

_____

What additional step(s) can I take to complete the healing that I have just journaled about in the above space? (ex: a phone call, letter, apology,etc.)

_____

_____

_____

_____

give

The gift of time, money, resources, or talent to an organization or person is both a powerful and practical way to help others.
What need comes to my mind -- today -- that I can find and fill and/or what person or organization needs a specific source of comfort or encouragement that I can give?

_____

_____

_____

_____

change

your

life

daily

date _____

talk to God

Today, in honest transparency, share -- in writing – your thoughts,
gratitude, regrets, fears, plans, hopes, dreams and requests
for yourself and others with the living, loving God.

s
p
i
r
i
t
u
a
l

_____

_____

_____

_____

_____

_____

_____

_____

_____

_____

_____

_____

_____

_____

_____

_____

_____

listen to God

God's voice is found in His word, the Bible.
Unless you have another system, read today's **change your life** Daily Bible
using Today's Date. Write in this area, any verse or verses that stand out,
touch your heart, encourage or correct you. **What is God saying to you today?**

_____

_____

_____

_____

_____

change
your
life
daily

date _____

m
e
n
t
a
l

detail your day

appointments

quiet time ☐
work out ☐
_____ ☐
_____ ☐
_____ ☐
_____ ☐
_____ ☐
_____ ☐
_____ ☐
_____ ☐
_____ ☐
_____ ☐
_____ ☐
_____ ☐
_____ ☐
_____ ☐
_____ ☐

calls to make   *phone #*

_____
_____
_____
_____

letters to write/fax/email
w   f   e
_____ ☐ ☐ ☐
_____ ☐ ☐ ☐
_____ ☐ ☐ ☐
_____ ☐ ☐ ☐

things to do

_____ ☐
_____ ☐
_____ ☐
_____ ☐
_____ ☐

define your dream

What is one practical step you can take toward reaching a goal -
and fulfilling a dream - in one or more areas of your life?
Use this space to brainstorm or to develop a dream that won't go away!

physical | emotional
mental | spiritual

change
your
life
daily

date _____

eat right

- · understand your own body type, genetics, metabolism, etc.
- · design a healthy, "plan ahead" eating plan that includes a balance of all the food groups in moderate portions
- · **record your daily intentions for meals and snacks below**
- · **review your progress and make daily adjustments**

breakfast	
lunch	
dinner	
snacks	

exercise regularly

- · determine what type of activity, where, when, how often and with whom you most like to exercise
- · develop a "week at a glance" exercise plan that includes a variety of 3 to 4 activities and has provision for alternate dates and times.

Detail your week plan; highlight today's plan.... what? when? where? with whom?

sun	mon	tue	wed	thur	fri	sat

journal

Journal below about any temptations, circumstances or emotions – today -- that might keep you from reaching your goals? (ex: vacation, celebrations, etc)

_____

_____

_____

_____

_____

_____

p
h
y
s
i
c
a
l

change
your
life
daily

date _____

e
m
o
t
i
o
n
a
l

forgive

To experience emotional balance on a daily basis, allow one or more of the below questions to prompt you to journal about the relationships in your life that need to heal and be healed.

Today, I know I need to ask _____ **to forgive me.**

I need to forgive myself for _____

I need to forgive _____ **for** _____

And I ask God to forgive me for _____

_____

_____

_____

_____

_____

_____

What additional step(s) can I take to complete the healing that I have just journaled about in the above space? (ex: a phone call, letter, apology,etc.)

_____

_____

_____

give

The gift of time, money, resources, or talent to an organization or person is both a powerful and practical way to help others.
What need comes to my mind -- today -- that I can find and fill and/or what person or organization needs a specific source of comfort or encouragement that I can give?

_____

_____

_____

_____

_____

change
your
life
daily

date _____

talk to God

Today, in honest transparency, share -- in writing – your thoughts,
gratitude, regrets, fears, plans, hopes, dreams and requests
for yourself and others with the living, loving God.

_____

_____

_____

_____

_____

_____

_____

_____

_____

_____

_____

_____

_____

_____

_____

_____

_____

_____

s
p
i
r
i
t
u
a
l

listen to God

God's voice is found in His word, the Bible.
Unless you have another system, read today's **change your life** Daily Bible
using Today's Date. Write in this area, any verse or verses that stand out,
touch your heart, encourage or correct you. **What is God saying to you today?**

_____

_____

_____

_____

_____

_____

change
your
life
daily

date _____

m
e
n
t
a
l

detail your day

appointments
quiet time	☐
work out	☐
	☐
	☐
	☐
	☐
	☐
	☐
	☐
	☐
	☐
	☐
	☐
	☐
	☐
	☐
	☐
	☐

calls to make   *phone #*

_____

_____

_____

_____

_____

letters to write/fax/email
w   f   e

_____ ☐ ☐ ☐

_____ ☐ ☐ ☐

_____ ☐ ☐ ☐

_____ ☐ ☐ ☐

things to do

_____ ☐

_____ ☐

_____ ☐

_____ ☐

_____ ☐

define your dream

What is one practical step you can take toward reaching a goal -
and fulfilling a dream - in one or more areas of your life?
Use this space to brainstorm or to develop a dream that won't go away!

physical | emotional

mental | spiritual

change

your

life

daily

date _____

eat right

· understand your own body type, genetics, metabolism, etc.
· design a healthy, "plan ahead" eating plan that includes a balance
  of all the food groups in moderate portions
· **record your daily intentions for meals and snacks below**
· **review your progress and make daily adjustments**

breakfast	
lunch	
dinner	
snacks	

exercise regularly

· determine what type of activity, where, when, how often and with whom you
  most like to exercise
· develop a "week at a glance" exercise plan that includes a variety of 3 to 4 activities
  and has provision for alternate dates and times.

Detail your week plan; highlight today's plan.... what? when? where? with whom?

sun	mon	tue	wed	thur	fri	sat

journal

**Journal below about any temptations, circumstances or emotions – today --
that might keep you from reaching your goals?** (ex: vacation, celebrations, etc)

_____

_____

_____

_____

_____

_____

p
h
y
s
i
c
a
l

change
your
life
daily

date _____

e

m

o

t

i

o

n

a

l

forgive

To experience emotional balance on a daily basis, allow one or more of the below questions to prompt you to journal about the relationships in your life that need to heal and be healed.

Today, I know I need to ask _____ **to forgive me.**

I need to forgive myself for _____

I need to forgive _____ **for** _____

And I ask God to forgive me for _____

_____

_____

_____

_____

_____

_____

_____

What additional step(s) can I take to complete the healing that I have just journaled about in the above space? (ex: a phone call, letter, apology,etc.)

_____

_____

_____

_____

give

The gift of time, money, resources, or talent to an organization or person is both a powerful and practical way to help others.
What need comes to my mind -- today -- that I can find and fill and/or what person or organization needs a specific source of comfort or encouragement that I can give?

_____

_____

_____

_____

_____

_____

change
your
life
daily

date _____

talk to God

Today, in honest transparency, share -- in writing – your thoughts, gratitude, regrets, fears, plans, hopes, dreams and requests for yourself and others with the living, loving God.

_____

_____

_____

_____

_____

_____

_____

_____

_____

_____

_____

_____

_____

_____

_____

_____

_____

s
p
i
r
i
t
u
a
l

listen to God

God's voice is found in His word, the Bible.
Unless you have another system, read today's **change your life** Daily Bible
using Today's Date. Write in this area, any verse or verses that stand out,
touch your heart, encourage or correct you. **What is God saying to you today?**

_____

_____

_____

_____

_____

change
your
life
daily

date _____

m
e
n
t
a
l

detail your day

appointments

quiet time ☐
work out ☐
_____ ☐
_____ ☐
_____ ☐
_____ ☐
_____ ☐
_____ ☐
_____ ☐
_____ ☐
_____ ☐
_____ ☐
_____ ☐
_____ ☐
_____ ☐
_____ ☐

calls to make   _phone #_

_____
_____
_____
_____
_____

letters to write/fax/email
                        w   f   e
_____ ☐   ☐   ☐
_____ ☐   ☐   ☐
_____ ☐   ☐   ☐
_____ ☐   ☐   ☐

things to do

_____ ☐
_____ ☐
_____ ☐
_____ ☐
_____ ☐

define your dream

What is one practical step you can take toward reaching a goal -
and fulfilling a dream - in one or more areas of your life?
Use this space to brainstorm or to develop a dream that won't go away!

physical | emotional
mental | spiritual

change
your
life
daily

date _____

eat right

- understand your own body type, genetics, metabolism, etc.
- design a healthy, "plan ahead" eating plan that includes a balance of all the food groups in moderate portions
- **record your daily intentions for meals and snacks below**
- **review your progress and make daily adjustments**

p
h
y
s
i
c
a
l

breakfast	
lunch	
dinner	
snacks	

exercise regularly

- determine what type of activity, where, when, how often and with whom you most like to exercise
- develop a "week at a glance" exercise plan that includes a variety of 3 to 4 activities and has provision for alternate dates and times.

Detail your week plan; highlight today's plan.... what? when? where? with whom?

sun	mon	tue	wed	thur	fri	sat

journal

Journal below about any temptations, circumstances or emotions – today -- that might keep you from reaching your goals? (ex: vacation, celebrations, etc)

_____

_____

_____

_____

_____

_____

change
your
life
daily

date _____

e
m
o
t
i
o
n
a
l

forgive

To experience emotional balance on a daily basis, allow one or more of the below questions to prompt you to journal about the relationships in your life that need to heal and be healed.

Today, I know I need to ask _____ **to forgive me.**

I need to forgive myself for _____

I need to forgive _____ **for** _____

And I ask God to forgive me for _____

_____

_____

_____

_____

_____

_____

What additional step(s) can I take to complete the healing that I have just journaled about in the above space? (ex: a phone call, letter, apology, etc.)

_____

_____

_____

_____

give

The gift of time, money, resources, or talent to an organization or person is both a powerful and practical way to help others.
What need comes to my mind -- today -- that I can find and fill and/or what person or organization needs a specific source of comfort or encouragement that I can give?

_____

_____

_____

_____

_____

change
your
life
daily

date _____

talk to God

Today, in honest transparency, share -- in writing – your thoughts, gratitude, regrets, fears, plans, hopes, dreams and requests for yourself and others with the living, loving God.

_____
_____
_____
_____
_____
_____
_____
_____
_____
_____
_____
_____
_____
_____
_____
_____
_____

s
p
i
r
i
t
u
a
l

listen to God

God's voice is found in His word, the Bible.
Unless you have another system, read today's **change your life Daily Bible** using Today's Date. Write in this area, any verse or verses that stand out, touch your heart, encourage or correct you. **What is God saying to you today?**

_____
_____
_____
_____
_____

change
your
life
daily

date _____

m
e
n
t
a
l

detail your day

appointments

quiet time ☐
work out ☐
_____ ☐
_____ ☐
_____ ☐
_____ ☐
_____ ☐
_____ ☐
_____ ☐
_____ ☐
_____ ☐
_____ ☐
_____ ☐
_____ ☐
_____ ☐
_____ ☐
_____ ☐

calls to make   *phone #*

_____
_____
_____
_____
_____
_____

letters to write/fax/email
w   f   e
_____ ☐ ☐ ☐
_____ ☐ ☐ ☐
_____ ☐ ☐ ☐
_____ ☐ ☐ ☐

things to do

_____ ☐
_____ ☐
_____ ☐
_____ ☐
_____ ☐

define your dream

What is one practical step you can take toward reaching a goal -
and fulfilling a dream - in one or more areas of your life?
Use this space to brainstorm or to develop a dream that won't go away!

physical | emotional
mental | spiritual

change
your
life
daily

date _____

eat right

- · understand your own body type, genetics, metabolism, etc.
- · design a healthy, "plan ahead" eating plan that includes a balance of all the food groups in moderate portions
- · **record your daily intentions for meals and snacks below**
- · **review your progress and make daily adjustments**

p
h
y
s
i
c
a
l

breakfast

lunch

dinner

snacks

exercise regularly

- · determine what type of activity, where, when, how often and with whom you most like to exercise
- · develop a "week at a glance" exercise plan that includes a variety of 3 to 4 activities and has provision for alternate dates and times.

Detail your week plan; highlight today's plan.... what? when? where? with whom?

sun	mon	tue	wed	thur	fri	sat

journal

Journal below about any temptations, circumstances or emotions – today -- that might keep you from reaching your goals? (ex: vacation, celebrations, etc)

change
your
life
daily

date _____

e

m

o

t

i

o

n

a

l

forgive

To experience emotional balance on a daily basis, allow one or more of the below questions to prompt you to journal about the relationships in your life that need to heal and be healed.

Today, I know I need to ask _____ **to forgive me.**

I need to forgive myself for _____

I need to forgive _____ **for** _____

And I ask God to forgive me for _____

_____

_____

_____

_____

_____

_____

What additional step(s) can I take to complete the healing that I have just journaled about in the above space? (ex: a phone call, letter, apology,etc.)

_____

_____

_____

_____

give

The gift of time, money, resources, or talent to an organization or person is both a powerful and practical way to help others.
What need comes to my mind -- today -- that I can find and fill and/or what person or organization needs a specific source of comfort or encouragement that I can give?

_____

_____

_____

_____

_____

change

your

life

daily

date _____

talk to God

Today, in honest transparency, share -- in writing – your thoughts, gratitude, regrets, fears, plans, hopes, dreams and requests for yourself and others with the living, loving God.

s
p
i
r
i
t
u
a
l

_____
_____
_____
_____
_____
_____
_____
_____
_____
_____
_____
_____
_____
_____
_____
_____
_____
_____

listen to God

God's voice is found in His word, the Bible.
Unless you have another system, read today's **change your life Daily Bible**
using Today's Date. Write in this area, any verse or verses that stand out,
touch your heart, encourage or correct you. **What is God saying to you today?**

_____
_____
_____
_____
_____
_____

change
your
life
daily

date _____

m
e
n
t
a
l

detail your day

appointments

quiet time ☐
work out ☐
☐
☐
☐
☐
☐
☐
☐
☐
☐
☐
☐
☐
☐
☐
☐
☐

calls to make *phone #*

_____
_____
_____
_____

letters to write/fax/email
w f e
☐ ☐ ☐
☐ ☐ ☐
☐ ☐ ☐
☐ ☐ ☐

things to do

_____ ☐
_____ ☐
_____ ☐
_____ ☐
_____ ☐

define your dream

What is one practical step you can take toward reaching a goal -
and fulfilling a dream - in one or more areas of your life?
Use this space to brainstorm or to develop a dream that won't go away!

| physical | emotional |
| mental | spiritual |

change
your
life
daily

date _____

eat right

- understand your own body type, genetics, metabolism, etc.
- design a healthy, "plan ahead" eating plan that includes a balance of all the food groups in moderate portions
- **record your daily intentions for meals and snacks below**
- **review your progress and make daily adjustments**

breakfast

_____

lunch

_____

dinner

_____

snacks

_____

exercise regularly

- determine what type of activity, where, when, how often and with whom you most like to exercise
- develop a "week at a glance" exercise plan that includes a variety of 3 to 4 activities and has provision for alternate dates and times.

Detail your week plan; highlight today's plan.... what? when? where? with whom?

sun	mon	tue	wed	thur	fri	sat

journal

Journal below about any temptations, circumstances or emotions – today -- that might keep you from reaching your goals? (ex: vacation, celebrations, etc)

_____

_____

_____

_____

_____

_____

p
h
y
s
i
c
a
l

change
your
life
daily

date _____

e
m
o
t
i
o
n
a
l

forgive

To experience emotional balance on a daily basis, allow one or more of the below questions to prompt you to journal about the relationships in your life that need to heal and be healed.

Today, I know I need to ask _____ **to forgive me.**

I need to forgive myself for _____

I need to forgive _____ **for** _____

And I ask God to forgive me for _____

_____

_____

_____

_____

_____

_____

What additional step(s) can I take to complete the healing that I have just journaled about in the above space? (ex: a phone call, letter, apology, etc.)

_____

_____

_____

_____

give

The gift of time, money, resources, or talent to an organization or person is both a powerful and practical way to help others.
What need comes to my mind -- today -- that I can find and fill and/or what person or organization needs a specific source of comfort or encouragement that I can give?

_____

_____

_____

_____

_____

change

your

life

daily

date _____

talk to God

Today, in honest transparency, share -- in writing – your thoughts, gratitude, regrets, fears, plans, hopes, dreams and requests for yourself and others with the living, loving God.

s
p
i
r
i
t
u
a
l

_____

_____

_____

_____

_____

_____

_____

_____

_____

_____

_____

_____

_____

_____

_____

_____

_____

_____

listen to God

God's voice is found in His word, the Bible.
Unless you have another system, read today's **change your life Daily Bible** using Today's Date. Write in this area, any verse or verses that stand out, touch your heart, encourage or correct you. **What is God saying to you today?**

_____

_____

_____

_____

_____

_____

change
your
life
daily

date _____

m
e
n
t
a
l

detail your day

appointments

quiet time ☐
work out ☐
_____ ☐
_____ ☐
_____ ☐
_____ ☐
_____ ☐
_____ ☐
_____ ☐
_____ ☐
_____ ☐
_____ ☐
_____ ☐
_____ ☐
_____ ☐
_____ ☐
_____ ☐

calls to make   *phone #*

_____
_____
_____
_____
_____

letters to write/fax/email
w   f   e
_____ ☐ ☐ ☐
_____ ☐ ☐ ☐
_____ ☐ ☐ ☐
_____ ☐ ☐ ☐

things to do

_____ ☐
_____ ☐
_____ ☐
_____ ☐
_____ ☐

define your dream

What is one practical step you can take toward reaching a goal -
and fulfilling a dream - in one or more areas of your life?
Use this space to brainstorm or to develop a dream that won't go away!

physical | emotional
mental | spiritual

change
your
life
daily

date _____

eat right

- understand your own body type, genetics, metabolism, etc.
- design a healthy, "plan ahead" eating plan that includes a balance of all the food groups in moderate portions
- **record your daily intentions for meals and snacks below**
- **review your progress and make daily adjustments**

breakfast	
lunch	
dinner	
snacks	

exercise regularly

- determine what type of activity, where, when, how often and with whom you most like to exercise
- develop a "week at a glance" exercise plan that includes a variety of 3 to 4 activities and has provision for alternate dates and times.

Detail your week plan; highlight today's plan.... what? when? where? with whom?

sun	mon	tue	wed	thur	fri	sat

journal

Journal below about any temptations, circumstances or emotions – today -- that might keep you from reaching your goals? (ex: vacation, celebrations, etc)

_____

_____

_____

_____

_____

_____

p h y s i c a l

change
your
life
daily

date _____

e

m

o

t

i

o

n

a

l

forgive

To experience emotional balance on a daily basis, allow one or more of the below questions to prompt you to journal about the relationships in your life that need to heal and be healed.

Today, I know I need to ask _____ **to forgive me.**

I need to forgive myself for _____

I need to forgive _____ **for** _____

And I ask God to forgive me for _____

_____

_____

_____

_____

_____

_____

What additional step(s) can I take to complete the healing that I have just journaled about in the above space? (ex: a phone call, letter, apology,etc.)

_____

_____

_____

_____

give

The gift of time, money, resources, or talent to an organization or person is both a powerful and practical way to help others.
What need comes to my mind -- today -- that I can find and fill and/or what person or organization needs a specific source of comfort or encouragement that I can give?

_____

_____

_____

_____

_____

_____

change

your

life

daily

date _____

talk to God

Today, in honest transparency, share -- in writing – your thoughts, gratitude, regrets, fears, plans, hopes, dreams and requests for yourself and others with the living, loving God.

s
p
i
r
i
t
u
a
l

_____

_____

_____

_____

_____

_____

_____

_____

_____

_____

_____

_____

_____

_____

_____

_____

_____

_____

_____

listen to God

God's voice is found in His word, the Bible.
Unless you have another system, read today's **change your life Daily Bible** using Today's Date. Write in this area, any verse or verses that stand out, touch your heart, encourage or correct you. **What is God saying to you today?**

_____

_____

_____

_____

_____

change
your
life
daily

date _____

m
e
n
t
a
l

detail your day

appointments

quiet time ☐
work out ☐
_____ ☐
_____ ☐
_____ ☐
_____ ☐
_____ ☐
_____ ☐
_____ ☐
_____ ☐
_____ ☐
_____ ☐
_____ ☐
_____ ☐
_____ ☐
_____ ☐
_____ ☐

calls to make   phone #

_____
_____
_____
_____
_____

letters to write/fax/email
                              w   f   e
_____ ☐ ☐ ☐
_____ ☐ ☐ ☐
_____ ☐ ☐ ☐
_____ ☐ ☐ ☐

things to do

_____ ☐
_____ ☐
_____ ☐
_____ ☐
_____ ☐

define your dream

What is one practical step you can take toward reaching a goal -
and fulfilling a dream - in one or more areas of your life?
Use this space to brainstorm or to develop a dream that won't go away!

physical | emotional

mental | spiritual

change
your
life
daily

date _____

eat right

- · understand your own body type, genetics, metabolism, etc.
- · design a healthy, "plan ahead" eating plan that includes a balance of all the food groups in moderate portions
- · **record your daily intentions for meals and snacks below**
- · **review your progress and make daily adjustments**

breakfast _____

lunch _____

dinner _____

snacks _____

exercise regularly

- · determine what type of activity, where, when, how often and with whom you most like to exercise
- · develop a "week at a glance" exercise plan that includes a variety of 3 to 4 activities and has provision for alternate dates and times.

Detail your week plan; highlight today's plan.... what? when? where? with whom?

sun	mon	tue	wed	thur	fri	sat

journal

Journal below about any temptations, circumstances or emotions – today -- that might keep you from reaching your goals? (ex: vacation, celebrations, etc)

_____

_____

_____

_____

_____

_____

p
h
y
s
i
c
a
l

change
your
life
daily

date _____

e

m

o

t

i

o

n

a

l

forgive

To experience emotional balance on a daily basis, allow one or more of the below questions to prompt you to journal about the relationships in your life that need to heal and be healed.

Today, I know I need to ask _____ **to forgive me.**

I need to forgive myself for _____

I need to forgive _____ **for** _____

And I ask God to forgive me for _____

_____

_____

_____

_____

_____

_____

What additional step(s) can I take to complete the healing that I have just journaled about in the above space? (ex: a phone call, letter, apology, etc.)

_____

_____

_____

_____

give

The gift of time, money, resources, or talent to an organization or person is both a powerful and practical way to help others.
What need comes to my mind -- today -- that I can find and fill and/or what person or organization needs a specific source of comfort or encouragement that I can give?

_____

_____

_____

_____

_____

change

your

life

daily

date _____

talk to God

Today, in honest transparency, share -- in writing – your thoughts,
gratitude, regrets, fears, plans, hopes, dreams and requests
for yourself and others with the living, loving God.

_____

_____

_____

_____

_____

_____

_____

_____

_____

_____

_____

_____

_____

_____

_____

_____

listen to God

God's voice is found in His word, the Bible.
Unless you have another system, read today's **change your life** Daily Bible
using Today's Date. Write in this area, any verse or verses that stand out,
touch your heart, encourage or correct you. **What is God saying to you today?**

_____

_____

_____

_____

_____

_____

change
your
life
daily

date _____

m
e
n
t
a
l

detail your day

appointments

quiet time	☐
work out	☐
	☐
	☐
	☐
	☐
	☐
	☐
	☐
	☐
	☐
	☐
	☐
	☐
	☐
	☐
	☐
	☐

calls to make   *phone #*

_____

_____

_____

_____

_____

_____

letters to write/fax/email
w   f   e

_____ ☐ ☐ ☐

_____ ☐ ☐ ☐

_____ ☐ ☐ ☐

_____ ☐ ☐ ☐

things to do

_____ ☐

_____ ☐

_____ ☐

_____ ☐

_____ ☐

define your dream

What is one practical step you can take toward reaching a goal -
and fulfilling a dream - in one or more areas of your life?
Use this space to brainstorm or to develop a dream that won't go away!

physical | emotional

mental | spiritual

change
your
life
daily

date _____

eat right

- understand your own body type, genetics, metabolism, etc.
- design a healthy, "plan ahead" eating plan that includes a balance of all the food groups in moderate portions
- **record your daily intentions for meals and snacks below**
- **review your progress and make daily adjustments**

p
h
y
s
i
c
a
l

breakfast _____

_____

lunch _____

_____

dinner _____

_____

snacks _____

exercise regularly

- determine what type of activity, where, when, how often and with whom you most like to exercise
- develop a "week at a glance" exercise plan that includes a variety of 3 to 4 activities and has provision for alternate dates and times.

Detail your week plan; highlight today's plan.... what? when? where? with whom?

sun	mon	tue	wed	thur	fri	sat

journal

Journal below about any temptations, circumstances or emotions – today -- that might keep you from reaching your goals? (ex: vacation, celebrations, etc)

_____

_____

_____

_____

_____

_____

change
your
life
daily

date _____

e
m
o
t
i
o
n
a
l

forgive

To experience emotional balance on a daily basis, allow one or more of the below questions to prompt you to journal about the relationships in your life that need to heal and be healed.

Today, I know I need to ask _____ **to forgive me.**

I need to forgive myself for _____

I need to forgive _____ **for** _____

And I ask God to forgive me for _____

_____

_____

_____

_____

_____

_____

_____

What additional step(s) can I take to complete the healing that I have just journaled about in the above space? (ex: a phone call, letter, apology,etc.)

_____

_____

_____

_____

give

The gift of time, money, resources, or talent to an organization or person is both a powerful and practical way to help others.
What need comes to my mind -- today -- that I can find and fill and/or what person or organization needs a specific source of comfort or encouragement that I can give?

_____

_____

_____

_____

_____

_____

change
your
life
daily

date _____

talk to God

Today, in honest transparency, share -- in writing – your thoughts, gratitude, regrets, fears, plans, hopes, dreams and requests for yourself and others with the living, loving God.

_____

_____

_____

_____

_____

_____

_____

_____

_____

_____

_____

_____

_____

_____

_____

_____

listen to God

God's voice is found in His word, the Bible.
Unless you have another system, read today's **change your life Daily Bible** using Today's Date. Write in this area, any verse or verses that stand out, touch your heart, encourage or correct you. **What is God saying to you today?**

_____

_____

_____

_____

_____

date _____

m
e
n
t
a
l

detail your day

appointments

- quiet time ☐
- work out ☐
- ☐
- ☐
- ☐
- ☐
- ☐
- ☐
- ☐
- ☐
- ☐
- ☐
- ☐
- ☐
- ☐
- ☐

calls to make   *phone #*

_____

_____

_____

_____

_____

letters to write/fax/email
w   f   e

_____ ☐ ☐ ☐

_____ ☐ ☐ ☐

_____ ☐ ☐ ☐

_____ ☐ ☐ ☐

things to do

_____ ☐

_____ ☐

_____ ☐

_____ ☐

_____ ☐

define your dream

What is one practical step you can take toward reaching a goal - and fulfilling a dream - in one or more areas of your life?
Use this space to brainstorm or to develop a dream that won't go away!

physical | emotional

mental | spiritual

change
your
life
daily

date _____

eat right

- · understand your own body type, genetics, metabolism, etc.
- · design a healthy, "plan ahead" eating plan that includes a balance of all the food groups in moderate portions
- · **record your daily intentions for meals and snacks below**
- · **review your progress and make daily adjustments**

breakfast	
lunch	
dinner	
snacks	

exercise regularly

- · determine what type of activity, where, when, how often and with whom you most like to exercise
- · develop a "week at a glance" exercise plan that includes a variety of 3 to 4 activities and has provision for alternate dates and times.

Detail your week plan; highlight today's plan.... what? when? where? with whom?

sun	mon	tue	wed	thur	fri	sat

journal

Journal below about any temptations, circumstances or emotions – today -- that might keep you from reaching your goals? (ex: vacation, celebrations, etc)

_____

_____

_____

_____

_____

p
h
y
s
i
c
a
l

change
your
life
daily

date _____

e
m
o
t
i
o
n
a
l

forgive

To experience emotional balance on a daily basis, allow one or more of the below questions to prompt you to journal about the relationships in your life that need to heal and be healed.

Today, I know I need to ask _____ **to forgive me.**

I need to forgive myself for _____

I need to forgive _____ **for** _____

And I ask God to forgive me for _____

_____

_____

_____

_____

_____

_____

_____

What additional step(s) can I take to complete the healing that I have just journaled about in the above space? (ex: a phone call, letter, apology, etc.)

_____

_____

_____

_____

give

The gift of time, money, resources, or talent to an organization or person is both a powerful and practical way to help others.
What need comes to my mind -- today -- that I can find and fill and/or what person or organization needs a specific source of comfort or encouragement that I can give?

_____

_____

_____

_____

_____

_____

change
your
life
daily

date _____

talk to God

Today, in honest transparency, share -- in writing – your thoughts, gratitude, regrets, fears, plans, hopes, dreams and requests for yourself and others with the living, loving God.

s
p
i
r
i
t
u
a
l

listen to God

God's voice is found in His word, the Bible.
Unless you have another system, read today's **change your life** Daily Bible using Today's Date. Write in this area, any verse or verses that stand out, touch your heart, encourage or correct you. **What is God saying to you today?**

change
your
life
daily

date _____

m
e
n
t
a
l

detail your day

appointments

quiet time	☐
work out	☐
	☐
	☐
	☐
	☐
	☐
	☐
	☐
	☐
	☐
	☐
	☐
	☐
	☐
	☐
	☐

calls to make   *phone #*

_____

_____

_____

_____

_____

letters to write/fax/email
w   f   e

_____ ☐ ☐ ☐

_____ ☐ ☐ ☐

_____ ☐ ☐ ☐

_____ ☐ ☐ ☐

things to do

_____ ☐

_____ ☐

_____ ☐

_____ ☐

_____ ☐

define your dream

What is one practical step you can take toward reaching a goal -
and fulfilling a dream - in one or more areas of your life?
Use this space to brainstorm or to develop a dream that won't go away!

physical | emotional
mental | spiritual

change

your

life

daily

date _____

eat right

- · understand your own body type, genetics, metabolism, etc.
- · design a healthy, "plan ahead" eating plan that includes a balance of all the food groups in moderate portions
- · **record your daily intentions for meals and snacks below**
- · **review your progress and make daily adjustments**

breakfast	
lunch	
dinner	
snacks	

p
h
y
s
i
c
a
l

exercise regularly

- · determine what type of activity, where, when, how often and with whom you most like to exercise
- · develop a "week at a glance" exercise plan that includes a variety of 3 to 4 activities and has provision for alternate dates and times.

Detail your week plan; highlight today's plan.... what? when? where? with whom?

sun	mon	tue	wed	thur	fri	sat

journal

Journal below about any temptations, circumstances or emotions – today -- that might keep you from reaching your goals? (ex: vacation, celebrations, etc)

_____

_____

_____

_____

_____

_____

change

your

life

daily

date _____

e

m

o

t

i

o

n

a

l

forgive

To experience emotional balance on a daily basis, allow one or more of the below questions to prompt you to journal about the relationships in your life that need to heal and be healed.

Today, I know I need to ask _____ **to forgive me.**

I need to forgive myself for _____

I need to forgive _____ **for** _____

And I ask God to forgive me for _____

_____

_____

_____

_____

_____

_____

What additional step(s) can I take to complete the healing that I have just journaled about in the above space? (ex: a phone call, letter, apology,etc.)

_____

_____

_____

give

The gift of time, money, resources, or talent to an organization or person is both a powerful and practical way to help others.
What need comes to my mind -- today -- that I can find and fill and/or what person or organization needs a specific source of comfort or encouragement that I can give?

_____

_____

_____

_____

_____

change

your

life

daily

date _____

talk to God

Today, in honest transparency, share -- in writing – your thoughts, gratitude, regrets, fears, plans, hopes, dreams and requests for yourself and others with the living, loving God.

_____

_____

_____

_____

_____

_____

_____

_____

_____

_____

_____

_____

_____

_____

_____

_____

_____

_____

s
p
i
r
i
t
u
a
l

listen to God

God's voice is found in His word, the Bible.
Unless you have another system, read today's **change your life** Daily Bible
using Today's Date. Write in this area, any verse or verses that stand out,
touch your heart, encourage or correct you. **What is God saying to you today?**

_____

_____

_____

_____

_____

_____

change
your
life
daily

date _____

m
e
n
t
a
l

detail your day

appointments

quiet time ☐

work out ☐

_____ ☐

_____ ☐

_____ ☐

_____ ☐

_____ ☐

_____ ☐

_____ ☐

_____ ☐

_____ ☐

_____ ☐

_____ ☐

_____ ☐

_____ ☐

_____ ☐

calls to make   *phone #*

_____

_____

_____

_____

letters to write/fax/email
   w   f   e
_____ ☐ ☐ ☐

_____ ☐ ☐ ☐

_____ ☐ ☐ ☐

_____ ☐ ☐ ☐

things to do

_____ ☐

_____ ☐

_____ ☐

_____ ☐

_____ ☐

define your dream

What is one practical step you can take toward reaching a goal -
and fulfilling a dream - in one or more areas of your life?
Use this space to brainstorm or to develop a dream that won't go away!

physical | emotional

mental | spiritual

change

your

life

daily

calendar

month

sunday	monday	tuesday	wednesday	thursday	friday	saturday

calendar

month

sunday	monday	tuesday	wednesday	thursday	friday	saturday

thoughts, ideas, requests, and dreams...

change
your
life
daily

thoughts, ideas, requests, and dreams...